THE C

Cefn-Bryntalch

Nigel and 'Covie' in 1938   Philip ('Peter Warlock')

*To Cynthia
with much love
from
Ian
10 June 94*

The Crying Curlew

Peter Warlock: Family & Influences
Centenary 1994

Ian Parrott

GOMER

First Impression—May 1994

© Ian Parrott

ISBN 1 85902 121 2

Printed by
J. D. Lewis & Sons Ltd., Gomer Press, Llandysul, Dyfed

To my friend, Patrick Mills,
Founder of the Peter Warlock Society

Contents

1. Introduction 9
   A half-Welsh composer's Centenary. Also 60 years
   after the deaths of Elgar, Delius and Holst.

2. Step-Family History & Shocks 15
   New information on his mother, Edith Covernton,
   and on the family of her second marriage to Walter
   Jones. Life at Cefn-Bryntalch, Abermule, Powys.

3. Suicide, Accident or—Murder? 34
   Various theories. Refutation of Cecil Gray.

4. Psychology and Magic 43
   Personality and influences on Philip.

5. Respectable Society 54
   Clashes between Philip and his family.

6. Wild Wales 65
   Sketch map and account of Philip's long walks.
   His interest in Celtic languages.

7. The Quarrelsome Warlock 78
   Why the limericks?

8. The Drunkard Myth & Final Thoughts 93
   Philip's hatreds and enthusiasms. An idol with feet
   of clay? The strength in his music.

Bibliography 107

Index 109

Acknowledgements

Robert Beckhard; Peter Boorman; Kenneth & Angela Bowen; Arthur Chater; Mrs. Christine Churchill; Christina Clarke; Mrs. Brenda Copley; Mrs. Betty Crawshaw; Mrs. Ann Crichton; Mrs. Riba Dugdale; Peter & Elaine English; Dr. David Evans; G. G. Evans; Dr. David Falla; Christopher Halliday; Mrs. Joann Healey; Nigel C. de R. Heseltine; Trevor Hold; Lady Hooson; Dr. D. Russell Hulme; The late Dr. Daniel Jones; Dr. G. Murray Jones; Phyllis Kinney; Rev. David Lockwood; Patrick Mills; Raymond Monk; Mrs. E. Nelson; Andrew Niell; Mrs. Joan Orr; Michael Parrott; Michael Pope; Jeremy Rye; Douglas W. Smith (Berriew); Fred Tomlinson; Professor J.E. Caerwyn Williams; Mrs. J. D. K. Williams; Dr. Kyffin Williams, R.A.

New pictures are by George A. Davies unless otherwise indicated.

My warm thanks go to Gillian Parry who prepared the manuscript for publication.

Thanks for financial assistance is acknowledged to The Margaret & Gwendoline Davies Charities, Raymond Monk and to friends who wish to remain anonymous.

1. Introduction

'O, Curlew, cry no more in the air'

W. B. Yeats

1994 sees the centenary of the birth of Philip Heseltine (pen-name Peter Warlock). It also marks 60 years after the deaths of Elgar, Delius and Holst.

The following thoughts are triggered mainly by the appearance at a late stage of Nigel Heseltine's revealing biography of his father.[1]

Philip Heseltine was born in London in 1894 and died in London just over 36 years later, but he was half Welsh and most of his best music was written at the geographical centre of Wales.

For many years the Peter Warlock Society had lost track of Nigel, his son. Finally, in 1991, he was discovered, having travelled to Western Australia. He was then promptly made a Vice-President of the Society.

In the *Oxford Companion to the Literature of Wales* (Oxford 1986), Nigel, described as poet and short-story writer, is said to have been born, 1916, at Montgomery. Now it appears from his own writing that he must have been born in London, farmed out to Camberley and then brought up from a tender age at his grandmother's home, Cefn-Bryntalch, near the village of Llandyssil, about half way between Montgomery and Abermule in Powys (then known as Montgomeryshire).

His book has many shocks in store and the title, *Capriol for Mother,* is somewhat enigmatic. The *Reader's Digest Great Illustrated Dictionary* of 1984 gives 'Capriole' as an upward leap in dressage of a horse or a jump in ballet, from the leap of a wild goat (*capriola* in Italian). Warlock's popular suite, *Capriol,* was based on old French dances. First as piano duet, 1926, then for strings, 1927, and finally for full orchestra, 1928, it was virtually his only full score. Taken by Curwen,

9

it had at first been rejected by another publisher as ineffective.[2] It was performed as a ballet in February 1930, the year of the composer's death, with choreography by Frederick Ashton.

We have not yet discovered the reason for the title, though we shall discover much about the hitherto elusive mother of the composer and her close relationship with her son. Indeed, David Cox, editor for many years of the *Peter Warlock Society Journal,* puts forward the suggestion of the composer symbolically dancing to the tune called by his mother over money. We must remember also that this lady was the biographer's grandmother.

Philip Heseltine was born at the Savoy Hotel, London, 30th October 1894. He joked that he was born on the Embankment,[3] much as Elgar enjoyed saying 'When I was at the Lunatic Asylum . . .' to put off sycophantic visitors.[4] (At the age of 22 Elgar had been appointed band instructor at the Pauper Lunatic Asylum at Powick.) Very little seems known about Philip's father, Arnold Heseltine, a successful solicitor, who 'died in 1897 when Philip was not yet three years old; six years later his mother remarried, when he was eight. She was then 43, and her new marriage brought her no more children (NH p.89)'. His 'excessively pious' father, Arnold Heseltine (born 1852), 'a younger son of a family of eleven, was a partner in a firm of solicitors.'[5] He died suddenly in March 1897 at the early age of 45. He had been previously married to Florence Marion Heseltine (formerly Hull), a sister of his brother Evelyn's wife, who died in 1880. Philip was then totally dependent on his mother, who seems to have roamed around a fair amount. The Savoy Hotel was not the only resplendent address, since we find Philip writing to her at the Hotel Brighton, Rue Rivoli, Paris, in April 1899. For his early childhood, he lived at 27 Hans Road, Chelsea, from which he attended school in Cliveden Place, Eaton Square; and he also started piano lessons. Many years later he returned to that part of Chelsea a much changed person.

In 1904 Philip became a bright pupil at Stone House Preparatory School in Broadstairs, a year after his mother had re-married Walter Buckley Jones. So the home from 1903 had become Cefn-Bryntalch, Abermule, though they kept on the Chelsea address for another seven years. The to-ing and fro-ing must have produced many sights, sounds and a new family at an impressionable age. For Philip, the father had left only a nebulous impression but with his stepfather, Walter Jones, a certain affinity was established at first, if only for a time. We will return later to the mother, Edith Covernton, born in Knighton in 1860, the daughter of a country doctor, who died in 1884 (NH p.39), her mother having died in 1870.

The composer's mother's full maiden name was Bessie Mary Edith Covernton but she soon became known affectionately as 'Covie' to her friends. To some she was known even as 'Aunt Covie'. Her grandfather emigrated from near London to Canada in 1810 and his son, Dr. Charles Covernton, settled later in Knighton. 'Covie', after a period with relations in Canada, became the second wife of Arnold Heseltine in 1891.

There is a view sometimes still held that great creative artists ought to be men of great moral stamina or even nobility. On this view the greater the composer the more he should be worshipped as a man of impeccable integrity if not down-right saintliness.

The idea is, of course, false. Let us, nevertheless, examine it.

Music-lovers fall into categories. They love first their hi-fi; then singers or players or conductors with TV-tested names; then orchestras or choirs. Then, at last, far down the list, are the composers, where priority is given to the 'great classical masters', thought of as gods descending from Parnassus and, especially in the case of Beethoven, looking rather like a heroic portrait of Napoleon by David. After them, the more modern composers trail far behind. For these we have three more types of music-lover: the worshipper, the enthusiast and the critical specialist.

Having been an active member for many years both of the Elgar Society and of the Peter Warlock Society,[6] I have been astonished at the very considerable amount of 'new material' on the lives of these two composers which has arisen in the sixty years since their deaths.

Recent speculations and revelations will have upset the complacent pictures built up by those who have got set in their ways. Conventional views of saints on pedestals have been toppled. I remember in particular an elderly Elgar-worshipper's reaction when the four hundred letters written to Alice Stuart-Wortley turned up. 'But they're *love*-letters,' he moaned, with heavy emphasis on the 'love'. Then, when Keith Alldrith's[7] historical novel, *Elgar on the Road to Hanley,* appeared in 1979, a new feminist view of the composer appeared. This, however, was superseded in 1983 by Michael de la Noy,[8] who presented the composer as many new things: an animal-hater rather than an animal-lover, a royalist fond of dressing up, rather than Percy Young's radical, etc. Moreover he hints that relationships with women could have been unsatisfactory as they were in the case of, say, Tchaikovsky or Brahms. The composer, he suggests, was rejected by his father and tied to his mother. Here we begin to find some sort of parallel with Philip Heseltine.

This Centenary picture represents not so much the homage of the author as of the subject: a man of impulsive enthusiasms, similar in this respect to Schumann, who 'discovered' other composers and writers. We may remind ourselves here of the Schumann-like understanding of poetry, not only to set to music but to act as a stimulus to literary work, for Philip was more than anything a superb song-writer.

'Hommage', spelt the French way with two ms, was a favourite word both of Philip and of van Dieren, whom he so much admired.

The basic view of Philip, to which we were all indoctrinated in different ways was to be found in Cecil Gray's *Memoir* of 1934.[9] We had no choice for many years. 'There has seldom been an artist' wrote Frank Baker two years later, 'whose life prompted so cunningly bad a book as Cecil Gray's—brilliantly as it was done.'[10] Yet, even with Gray's emphasis on a split personality, at least we were given a positive character; not the 19th-century-style saint to whom we made obeisance, to be sure, but at least stable and reliable. We preferred reading of the beard-pointing, swashbuckling, ale-swigging extrovert to the melancholy, dreaming introvert, but were ill-prepared for what was to follow in the years to come. Fred Tomlinson[11] and Dr. Ian Copley,[12] who died on 24 December 1988, amongst many others, have gradually stripped away much of what now looks like hero-worship. Denis ApIvor,[13] also, has given us a recent study of the personality. Many enthusiasts, however, were knocked sideways by the new bombshell, the memoir of his son, which, although started in 1956, actually appeared in 1992,[14] when 'everyone concerned is dead', so there could be no backlash.

Of the Heseltine side of the family not a great deal more can be said here except to note that the several rich uncles did not help the young composer very much, their riches gradually fading away. The colourful 'Uncle Joe' (Arthur Heseltine) lived in the next village to Grez-sur-Loing, however, and he deserves to be remembered for introducing Philip to Delius before the outbreak of the First War (NH p.42 *et seq*).

Uncle Joe was a painter who had won the Rome Scholarship at the age of 19 and was later a trustee of the National Gallery (NH p.96) and, having married a French wife, settled in France, a correspondence with Philip starting in 1908. This contact proved to be of great significance in the build-up of the future composer. At first Philip was a schoolboy who paid homage to older creative artists. Then, with later attractions, he was slowly and painfully to grow out of such dependencies. His first attempt as a music critic was an article on Schönberg (quite a revolutionary gesture) for the *Musical Standard* in

13

1912 (NH p.63) and, with advice from Sorabji and others he continued this line, including becoming for a few months in 1915 a music critic for the *Daily Mail*.[15]

The long-lived Kaikosru Sorabji dedicated his huge *Piano Concerto*, Op. 3, to Philip in 1916.

We should remember that Philip grew up at a time of violent upheavals in the overseas musical world. 1913 was the year of riots over Stravinsky's *Rite of Spring* in Paris and Schönberg and his school in Vienna.

[1] Heseltine, Nigel, *Capriol for Mother: A Memoir of Philip Heseltine (Peter Warlock) and his family by his son,* (Thames Publishing 1992). Page numbers in brackets refer to this book.

[2] Copley, I. A., *The Music of Peter Warlock: A Critical Survey* (Dennis Dobson 1979), p. 236.

[3] Gray, Cecil, *Peter Warlock. A Memoir of Philip Heseltine* (Jonathan Cape 1934), p. 33.

[4] Young, Percy, *Elgar O. M. A Study of a Musician* (Collins 1955), p. 46.

[5] Information kindly supplied by Barry Smith in a letter of 5 September 1993.

[6] Ian Parrott has been a vice-president of the former since 1973 and of the latter since 1984.

[7] Alldrith, K., *Elgar on the Road to Hanley* (André Deutsh 1979).

[8] De la Noy, Michael, *Elgar: The Man* (Allen Lane 1983).

[9] Gray, *op.cit.*

[10] Baker, Frank, 'The Artist's Private Life' in *The Chesterian,* November-December 1936.

[11] Tomlinson, Fred, *A Peter Warlock Handbook* (Triad Press, Vol.I 1974, Vol.II 1977).

[12] Copley, *op.cit.*

[13] Aplvor, Denis, 'Philip Heseltine: a Psychological Study' (*Music Review,* May 1985).

[14] Heseltine, Nigel, *op.cit.*

[15] Tomlinson, *op.cit.*

2. Step-Family History & Shocks

Six years after Philip's father, Arnold, had died, the wealthy widow (who had been Arnold's second wife) remarried.

Not a word about this dominant and dominating lady, except once at the inquest, appears in Gray, who doesn't even bother to put her in the Index. Yet she had the most powerful influence over her son. Born Edith Covernton, she was to be known as 'Covie'. Her second husband, Walter Jones, was a son of Richard Edward Jones, who died 20th April 1916, descendant of Mochdre hill-farmers who provided flannel for the Newtown market. Richard designed Cefn-Bryntalch in 1864 and the building was completed by 1869. The architect, Bodley, was more used to designing churches than this red-brick mansion, with its five and a half acres of land, tennis court and croquet lawn. The tennis court was behind the croquet lawn. An unusual architectural feature of the house is the double storey porch and there are two fine Palladian windows. There were, according to Philip, 'a dozen empty rooms' to himself[1] and four or five maids. There was also a Norman motte-and-bailey fort in the Castle wood behind the house.

Cefn-Bryntalch—croquet lawn at back.

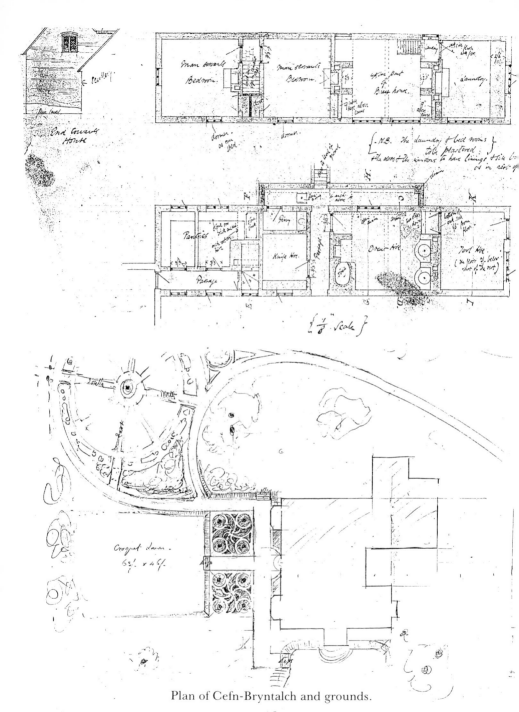

Plan of Cefn-Bryntalch and grounds.

16

Palladian window.

Richard Edward and Catherine Jones with pony and trap outside Cefn-Bryntalch, 1876. *By courtesy of Mr. Jeremy Rye.*

17

The architectural drawings of Cefn-Bryntalch made for S. J. Bodley in January 1864 show some interesting features. On one, Mr. A. Chamberlain of 390 Harley Street, London, has written, 'If Mr. Jones likes it, it will be much better to have all the timber work of oak.' Then, on a sketch of the roof over the kitchen, we read, 'None but cut wrought iron nails to be used.' From Elizabeth Longford's memoirs it may possibly be deduced that this was the Arthur Chamberlain, related by marriage to John Nettlefield of Birmingham, who saw a new screw at the Great Exhibition of 1851 and whose brother-in-law, Joseph Chamberlain, put up most of the capital for a new screw factory. Lady Longford herself was born at 108 Harley Street, the daughter of Dr. Bishop N. Harman, 'her mother being a Chamberlain'.[2]

So clearly Richard Edward Jones was not used to having things done by halves.

Four years earlier, when resident at the Rock, Newtown, he had acted as one of the executors for the will of Richard Owens, who was a member of another wealthy family later to be known for its financial advice to the Davies sisters of Gregynog, then part of the estate of Baron Sudeley, who, also in 1860, appointed Richard a Lieutenant in the First Montgomeryshire Rifle Volunteers. His son, Walter (Philip's step-father), was to follow this line as well as becoming a J.P. and visiting magistrate to the lunatic asylum. Shades of young Elgar twenty years earlier and only 50 miles away! In a letter from South Africa of February 1902, the brother, Lumley, wrote 'The idea of Walter a magistrate is too funny for words.' (see below).

Cefn-Bryntalch, when Richard took over, with its 30 rooms, had two carriage houses, several stables, loose box, and out-houses—sufficient for no less than 23 horses. There were 22 servants and 2 governesses—and a brew house!

Walter was the eldest of seven children. As well as four sisters, there were two brothers: Whitmore, a colonel, and Lumley, who reached the exalted rank of brigadier-general

18

(NH p.127). When young Philip was growing up in Hans Road, Chelsea, starting piano lessons and first school in Cliveden Place, Eaton Square, his step-uncles-to-be, Lumley and Whitmore, were in far-flung parts of the Empire: first in India and Burma and later, after the Boer War had broken out (1899) in South Africa. Lumley sailed from Bombay to Durban in December 1901. His letters to his mother, Catherine Jones,[3] are to a considerable extent filled with accounts of shooting, or nearly shooting, elephants and tigers in Burma in 1899. '. . . followed two tuskers . . . a beautiful tiger about 60 yards away . . . shot him with my carbine . . . my tracker was carrying my 8 bore,' etc.

The letter of Lumley, now a company commander in South Africa, of 26th January 1902, after a great deal on the capture and loss of horses and on the advance to engage the Boers, states laconically, 'I got a letter from Walter,' and his letter of 7th February, after details of how some Boers had been shot, adds, as a P.S., that he thought the idea of Walter being a magistrate was funny. It looks as if Walter was a somewhat gentle figure, the impression confirmed two generations later by Nigel in his book (NH p.92). Lumley's opinion of his brother, Whitmore (who had also been in South Africa), is given in a letter of 20th May 1902, a month before Peace was declared. His mother had said that 'Whit' was better and more cheerful. This was a bad sign, wrote his brother, as 'he is always at his best when he has a real good grouse on.'

As can be seen on a plaque in Llandyssil church, Walter died on 13th January 1938, and the gravestone asks us 'with love to remember him'. He was 74. His brother, Brigadier-General Lumley Owen Williames Jones, D.S.O., the step-uncle who 'provided the necessary military prestige' (NH p.127) in the War in 1917, had died on 14th September 1918 of Spanish flu. This had been after getting through the War unscathed. Philip was told about Lumley's escapades by his mother and, in a letter of 26th December 1914, dutifully

19

expressed his admiration (in spite of his convictions, see below, p. 56), 'I am so glad Lumley was able to return for Christmas. What an incredibly frightful time he must have had—and what marvellous escapes—it is too terrible.'[4] In this church, Philip was called upon in November 1921 to play for a service, because the regular organist—irony of ironies —was drunk. A letter, somewhat expurgated, to Cecil Gray, describing the event, appears in the latter's biography.[5] The outgoing voluntary on Tôn-y-Botel (see below, p. 78) made a somewhat Bach-like impression in that the congregation were confounded by his strange harmonies. The church was lit by electricity installed in memory of Richard.

'Covie' inserted the name Buckley from Walter's mother, Catherine Buckley-Williames. Catherine, who died 5th April 1915, was descended from Rice Pryce Buckley Williames, 1802-1871, himself descended from the Pryces of Newtown and the Buckleys of Dolfor.[6] So 'Covie' became known as Mrs Buckley Jones. With Walter and young Philip she moved shortly after her second marriage to Cefn-Bryntalch, Abermule. Here, from when Philip started at Eton in 1908, 'Covie' received shock after shock as Philip, growing up, went against all her wishes.

Many early experiences must have left their mark on a boy without a father who had become a 'mother's darling'. She tried to give him always what he wanted, even to the extent of sending a copy of the Apocrypha in 1906, though this must have seemed decidedly odd at the time.

His precocious intellectual ability, appreciated by Stone House with spectacular promotions and later by individual 'crammer' tutors, may not have been so well channelled at the public school. The OTC camp in 1910 and the probable bullying and possible homosexuality may have added to the unpleasantness. Even Christ Church, Oxford, appears to have become uncongenial, as he became more of a misfit, living then in a Delius-dominated world of his own.

1897

1911

1912

1921 (wearing Tunisian djellaba).

Photographs of Philip Heseltine.

By courtesy of Nigel Heseltine.

'Covie' and Walter, 1906-7.

'Covie' c.1908.

Philip clearly loathed Eton with its hearty adolescent bawling of Victorian hymns in an all-male college chapel. A mercilessly satirical caricature of this public school style of singing appears in the opening pages of *Antic Hay* by Aldous Huxley (1894-1963), another protestor, who went to Eton and Oxford, whom Philip was to meet again at the same time as D. H. Lawrence in 1915.

Philip felt irked by such an extrovert masculine world, into which he must have fitted most inadequately. Yet it made its impact in an unexpected way later on when he wrote several fine drinking songs for male voices, suggesting they be 'roared over mugs of beer'.[7] Whether for high or low voice he didn't mind and on the high voice version of *Good Ale* (1922) he wrote 'for roaring unaccompanied it doesn't matter'. His wit came out also at the end of this song when before the final 'Prestissimo' he wrote in brackets: 'Hey'. These songs may have been a cover-up for his essentially unhappy nature but the musical results were often of a very high order. One of the most popular, a Masefield setting called *Captain Stratton's Fancy* of 1920, marked 'with great heartiness', he described as a 'true toper's tune to troll with trulls and trollops in a tavern'. In this he digs with gusto at serious concerts as he sets the words:

O some are fond of fiddles and a song well sung
And some are all for music for to lilt upon the tongue,
But mouths were made for tankards and for sucking at the bung,
Says the old, bold mate of Henry Morgan.

And when, at the end of his life, he wrote *The Cricketers of Hambledon,* it seems as if he is almost back at school with an 'after games' beano.

He left Eton at 16; dropped out of Oxford without a degree; and in 1914 managed to drop out of London University without completing even a first year (NH pp. 41, 52 and 82). This is not exactly the style of a normal elegant biography with its 'educated at Eton and read classics at Oxford'. In his mother's mind was a brilliant career in the Civil Service for the future 'Sir' Philip Heseltine (NH p.53), squire of Bryntalch and other estates (NH p.91). Instead, Philip associated with a series of 'unsuitable' companions, coming under the influence of hard, strong personalities: D. H. Lawrence, the 'Master' (NH p.125), and Bernard van Dieren, a 'guiding personality' (NH p.81); and, in particular to be admired, Delius (NH p.52), and Bartók, of which 'there was little that was human . . . and nothing that was weak' (NH p.149). Strangely, Cecil Gray, near the end of his life, came round to a similar view: 'Béla Bartók, in short, was completely inhuman. . .' but 'he was pure spirit'.[8]

Percy Young makes pertinent references in his *History of British Music*. Philip 'found education at Eton and Oxford uncongenial in the extreme' and in effect was 'self-taught in music'.[9] This might be thought similar to Elgar, were it not that he was well-off, while Elgar was from a poor background. Philip, continues Dr. Young, was 'ill-equipped for dealing with the normal problems of life . . . in his art, however, he discovered the secret of co-ordination and of orderliness . . . (He) had a Schubertian talent for discovering the figurative impulses proper to a particular song.' This was despite his 'consciously antique country fancies'.[10]

Since the present author, also a composer, went to Harrow —generally considered comparable with Philip's prestigious public school—it may be agreed that 'uncongenial in the extreme' for a sensitive artistic temperament is no exaggeration.

'I'm not sure if I want to "get on"', Philip once said very quietly to his mother (NH p.160).

Philip was now 'unemployable', having integrated himself with a band right outside orthodox society (NH p.307). His association with at least three unloved women produced two children. One, born 13 July 1916, who died in infancy, was the offspring of Minnie Lucy (Bobbie), née Channing ('Puma', 1898-1942), to whom Philip was officially married on 22 December 1916 but from whom he wished always

24

afterwards to escape. It seems that 'Covie' took on the responsibility of looking after the infant, who was called Peter. When Peter was scarcely one year old, Puma wrote from Dublin, 1st October 1917, to 'Dear Philip's Mother', expressing her relief that she was no longer 'with Child again' and talking of the shoes that Peter, her baby, might wear. 'I expect you know best,' she wrote. 'Anyway, I suppose he will have to wear shoes sometime,' she continued with undomesticated indifference. She then referred to Philip's feet which 'don't look as if they have ever suffered from cramp' and extolled the virtues of Cork-made brogues. After 'Yours affectionately Puma', she just remembered to add, 'P.S. I am longing to know that Peter is safe with you.'[11] In 1915 Philip, with other artists, had gone to Garsington Manor, the home of Philip and Lady Ottoline Morrell. Lady Ottoline was an imaginative photographer, as her picture at this time of two naked girls, 'Cavorting by the Pool', shows. It is of her daughter, Julian, and her cousin, Lalage. It was customary at this time to have a nanny or governess and the self-willed Julian, now aged 9 and lacking parental control, was good at getting her own way, whoever was employed. One would imagine that there will have been quite a turn-over of such nannies, some of them from Switzerland.

Philip's other child was half Swiss, the mother being a friend of Juliette Baillot, one-time governess to this spoilt daughter, and later Mrs. Julian Huxley. The child, called Nigel, was cared for by a family called Halliday in Camberley until 'salvaged' by 'Covie' (NH p.123). He, the surviving son, is the author of this 'curiously moving memoir', as Michael Kennedy describes it. In his review, Kennedy curtly remarks that Philip was a 'bad picker of women'. He thought, moreover, that the mother was right to ascribe his unhappiness to his 'failure to fit himself into the world in which he was brought up'.[12] In the case of both children, it seems that the father's, not the mother's, family was left 'holding the baby'. So, although it was not the usual custom, the long-suffering

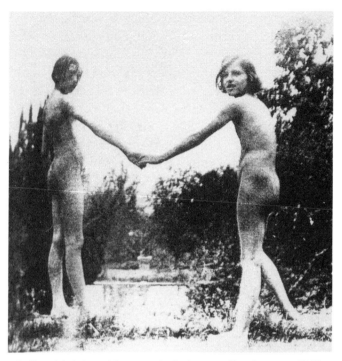

Julian (right) and her cousin Lalage at Garsington, 1915.

grandmother, 'Covie', took on the responsibility of subsequent upbringing.

Nigel was treated somewhat as a pet by Walter and 'Covie'. After the trauma of the death first of the other child, Peter, and then, catastrophically, of Philip himself (when Nigel was 14), both parents, no doubt by way of compensation, tended to pamper the grandson. I am told by a local source that in his teens Nigel was 'spoilt' and became too self-confident for his years. This was only to have been expected, but he mellowed.

At the same time, even after years of unravelling the supposed dedicatees in Elgar's 'Enigma' *Variations* and *Violin Concerto,* we come up once more against new theories on *his* life. We knew Lady Mary Lygon had jostled for position with Rosa Burley and then with Helen Weaver, etc. Now Michael Kennedy comes up with the idea that 'a composer who had always seemed the epitome of English respectability . . . had fathered an illegitimate child', after an affair with a Mrs. Nelson (*Sunday Telegraph,* 15th November 1992). Another blow, I fear, for my aged Elgar-worshipper.

Philip Heseltine had 'either to be worshipping a *maitre* or trying to lord it over his inferiors', says his son, '. . . accusations of impotence are thrown about, notably at D. H. Lawrence, since he had a squeaky voice and wrote much about sex' (NH p. 114). Dr. Copley confirms that Philip was 'decidedly prone to hero-worship and discipleship', especially at the time of this 'turbulent friendship',[13] his relationship with Lawrence, 1885-1930, being a 'combination of female submission and filial revolt' (NH p. 112). David Herbert Lawrence was much affected by the death of his mother to whom he had been abnormally close. This relationship seems similar to that of Philip, whose letters to his own mother up to the age of 10 had shown an effusively sentimental attachment.[14] To his mother, in May 1904 for example, Philip was her 'VERY loving Wooley, Wooley, Lambkin'.

Much valuable information is given by Dr. Copley's study, *A Turbulent Friendship* of 1983, which should be read again.

According to a recent paperback on him by Jeffrey Meyers, Lawrence seems to have had a homosexual relationship with a Cornish farmer,[15] which confirms Gray's oblique references. Lawrence was the then controversial novelist on whom Philip lavished so much of his ineffective enthusiasm—as well as his family headed notepaper and money—trying early in 1916 to promote *The Rainbow* (a year after it had been suppressed as obscene). A circular was printed at his 'only stable address', hoping for the 'love of the quest of truth in this country, underneath all the smug moral assurance, the unspeakably loathsome acquiescence in the existing social system',[16] but the response was totally inadequate—and Lawrence pretended that it was unimportant. The wordy protest of this letter is not unlike the final lines of *The Rainbow* with its 'world built up in a living fabric of Truth, fitting to the over-arching of heaven'. Philip came off badly bruised from knowing and helping this odd, ungrateful 'distorted thinker' (as he called Lawrence in a letter to Delius of April 1916), whom he later detested.

Although a recent book on Lady Ottoline[17] makes lavish reference to many artists entertained at Garsington, such as D. H. Lawrence, Aldous Huxley and Augustus John, the only meagre mention of Philip Heseltine reveals that Ottoline found him 'so degenerate that he seems somehow corrupt'. A dismissive footnote states that, being involved in satanism, he 'significantly took the name of Peter Warlock for his short career as a composer of songs and airs, the best known being a Yeats cycle, *The Curlew.*' This damning with faint praise makes one ask if there could have been smoke without fire.

After Cornwall with Lawrence, Philip's year in Ireland, 1917-18, was not, as Gray maintained, the occasion for 'finding himself' as a composer.[18] He was there for 'healing' (NH p. 136)—as well he might be by this time. He had spent much time studying Celtic languages (see below) and also the theory of magic in the writings of Eliphas Lévi (who had also been studied—see below—by Crowley) which was based on Abra-Melin the Magus who in 1458 had propounded a system similar to yoga.

Philip became an enthusiast for many composers and we have seen that in the case of Delius his feelings were virtually those of a hero-worshipper. He was much taken up by the music of van Dieren and, in his last letter to him of 14th September 1928, he was still somewhat fulsome by referring to the latter's composition as 'that superlatively lovely quartet'.[19] He was discerning in the case of Bartók. In fact, young Philip had been unusually perceptive about this as yet unknown 'modernist'. In November 1920 Bartók had written, though he had not yet met him, telling Philip that since 1912 his publishers had refused to take on any more. Considered unacceptably 'new', Bartók was forced into reproducing some of his music privately.[20] In any case Philip already knew much of the music before Universal took over any of it in 1918, since Bartók's brand new piano music had been introduced to him at Eton by his far-sighted music teacher, Colin Taylor, in 1908. If teachers deserve mention, then Colin Taylor should be remembered for his formative influence.

Philip stayed with Bartók on a visit to Budapest in April 1921, and invited him to Cefn-Bryntalch in 1922—he was on to a winner this time[21]—and got Bartók to contribute to his magazine, *The Sackbut.*

On the invitation of the Gregynog Professor of Music, Sir Walford Davies (helped by another famous Hungarian, the violinist, dedicatee of Bartók's *Violin Sonata No. 2,* Jelly d'Arányi),[22] Bartók played in a concert at the University College of Wales, Aberystwyth, on Thursday, 16th March, 1922. Even though he included nothing more revolutionary to modern ears than the *Bear Dance* and *Allegro Barbaro* (1911), Bartók's percussive style at the keyboard created a sensation. Walford Davies, who had introduced the unknown Hungarian with his customary authority, was heard afterwards to comment, 'Baffling, isn't it?'.[23] The distinguished Aberystwyth musician, Charles Clements, 1898-1983, who 'turned over', admired Bartók's playing in the Beethoven *'Archduke'* Trio with Hubert Davies, violin, and Arthur Williams, cello. Others found the percussively-played new music strange or absurdly amusing.

Before leaving Aberystwyth, Bartók sent a telegram from the Music Department to Philip, expecting to be met at Abermule. According to the son, the visit was on the night *before* the concert (NH p. 158), but here is Bartók's letter of 12th March:

12 March 1922

Dear Mr. Heseltine,

Thank you for your letter. You may inquire after me at the Music House (University College of Wales) in Aberystwyth, if you wish to come to the concert. They will tell you all about the

29

arrangements—I can come to Abermule only after the concert which will take place on the 16th. Perhaps we could go together to Abermule. I prefer to take the train, unless the auto is closed. I am so much looking forward to seeing you again.

Yours very sincerely,
BARTOK.

Cecil Gray heard the great Hungarian violinist, Jelly d'Arányi, play Bartók's new sonata with the composer in London on 14th March. In a letter to Philip he called her, with clod-hopping humour, the 'Orange jelly'. In his letter of 13th March[24] he wrote that Bartók 'will be packed up and delivered to you on Wednesday—in a plain wrapper.' That means, in fact, on the day before the concert in Aberystwyth.

Bartók with Jelly d'Arányi (left) and Adila Fachiri (née Arányi). London, March 1922. This photograph originally appeared in the *Daily Sketch,* 24 March 1922.

(from 'Bartók in Britain' by Malcolm Gillies, O.U.P. 1989)
by permission of the Oxford University Press.

Either way, it may be assumed that he was met at Abermule station by Boss-eye Stevens in a glass-fronted fly (NH p. 158). It is fortunate that Bartók was not travelling a year earlier on his remarkable visit. On 26th January 1921 (eight months before Philip had returned to Cefn-Bryntalch from his year of travelling) the one-track railway, with its supposedly foolproof system of signalling, had been the scene of a head-on collision near Abermule, seventeen people being killed.

After this disaster, several railway workers were sacked, having been drinking at the Abermule Hotel, then run by Boss-eye Stevens. Ernest Stevens, having lost an eye in the Newtown foundry, wore a glass one and was known locally as 'Boss'. He drove three vehicles, one being a covered carriage in which he used to drive 'Covie' to church at Llandyssil. He would meet visitors at the station and sometimes take them out for rides. On Tuesdays he would drive into Newtown, when he usually got drunk. After a while he switched to running the nearby Waterloo Arms, living on into his nineties. Visitors in the post-horse-drawn era were met by car by another colourful character known as Tom Cooper.

The first of Philip's *Folk-Song Preludes* for piano ties up with his lecture in the Abbey Theatre, Dublin, 12th May 1918, called 'What Music Is'. Its more than usually acid harmonies in the last line suggest Bartók's early *Bear Dance* style, which was already well known, since he included Bartók in his lecture. It is likely also that, on his visit to Wales four years later, Bartók astounded not only the good people of Aberystwyth but the parents and son at Cefn-Bryntalch as well. No doubt the prudish Walford Davies, no less than 'Covie', would have been suitably horrified, had they realised that this hard-hitting Hungarian had recently completed a ballet, *The Miraculous Mandarin,* which was to be 'taken off' in Cologne, 1926, and cancelled in Prague and Budapest because it was about a macabre prostitute.

This sort of thing was happening in Britain to modern books, modern plays and modern paintings as well as to music; and it was in this world of protest to Victorian values that Philip was living. But the gentry and would-be gentry of mid-Wales were behind the times, so the cultural gap was that much the greater.

Philip's enthusiasm for van Dieren's music seems to have been less well placed. Soon after van Dieren had died in April 1936, attempts were made, as I remember, to put on his opera, *The Tailor,* at Oxford, but after this had failed to materialise, his compositions have gradually faded from view.

Philip's mother, who had been 'tricked' into providing Gray with letters from Delius and others, etc., for his biography (NH p. 21), described Gray as resembling 'a fat, white slug' (NH p. 113). The son, who endorsed this description, thought of him as a ponderous buffoon; and it is clear that the resultant biography is wildly misleading in many respects. Anthony Powell[25] saw Gray as 'a plump bespectacled rather unforthcoming Scot', whose daughter thought he practised black magic.

Nigel Heseltine refers to a Mrs. Onslow (NH p. 20), who warned him not to read Gray's biography. This lady can be identified as Mrs. Mabel Onslow, of a Devon family, who married Arthur Loftus Onslow, mining engineer. They lived at Mount Severn, Llanidloes, he being High Sheriff for Montgomeryshire in 1936. Two of their three sons were killed in the Abermule railway disaster. Mrs. Onslow, an amateur water colour artist, wore colourful clothes and 'floppy' hats. Also she was a keen conservationist and vegetarian. Her advice to Lady Hooson's mother, on decorating her house in Llanidloes, reads almost like poetry which would probably have appealed to Philip: a room to be 'a forest in autumn . . . underfoot red brown earth . . . the curtains the sunset glow so rich and bright . . . the woodwork the tree stems . . . sofas like copper beech leaves.' The image of the art of Delius, thought Philip, was 'to be seen in the rich colours of the sunset fires'.[26]

[1] Gray, *op.cit.*
[2] Longford, Elizabeth, *Memoirs. The Pebbled Shore* (Weidenfeld & Nicholson 1986).
[3] Spelt Katharine in *Montgomery Collections* Vol.IX. She married Richard in 1875.
[4] Brit. Lib. ADD MS 57,961.
[5] *Ibid.,* p. 244.
[6] Williams, Richard, *Montgomeryshire Worthies* (London 1875).
[7] *The Choral Music of Peter Warlock,* two vols., introduced by Fred Tomlinson and sponsored by Ruddles Brewery (Thames, 1990).
[8] Gray, Cecil, *Musical Chairs* (London 1948).
[9] Young, Percy M., *A History of British Music,* (Benn 1967), p. 576.
[10] *Ibid.,* p. 474.
[11] Brit. Lib. ADD MS 57,961.
[12] Kennedy, Michael, *Sunday Telegraph,* 7th February 1993.
[13] Copley, I. A., *A Turbulent Friendship—A Study of the Relationship Between D. H. Lawrence and Philip Heseltine* (Thames 1983).
[14] Brit. Lib. ADD MS 57,958.
[15] Meyers, Jeffrey, *D. H. Lawrence* (Papermac 1993). See also Gray, *op.cit.,* pp. 114 and 119.
[16] Letter to Olivia (Viva) Smith, 16 February 1916.
[17] Seymour, Miranda, *Ottoline Morrell, Life on the Grand Scale* (Hodder 1992).
[18] Gray, *Peter Warlock, op.cit.,* p. 158.
[19] Tomlinson, Fred, *Warlock and van Dieren* (Thames 1978).
[20] Szigeti, letter, *'Bartók's Early Struggles' (Performing Right, No. 44, April 1966).*
[21] See Heseltine, Philip, 'Modern Hungarian Composers' (*Musical Times,* 1 March 1922).
[22] Jelly, with her sister Adila, had been part of Ottoline Morrell's company at Garsington. At that time striking, passionate and raven-haired, she subsequently played several times at Gregynog festivals. Later still, I had the pleasure of conducting for her and her sister. In 1937 Szigeti's arrangement of three movements from *Capriol* (Basse-danse, Pavane and Mattachins) for violin and piano were published in New York by Carl Fischer. The dedication was 'To Jelly d'Arányi and Adila Fachiri' (see *P. W. Society Newsletter* 51, Autumn 1993, p. 14).
[23] Gillies, Malcolm, *Bartók in Britain* (O.U.P. 1989), p. 34. Also pp. 115-130.
[24] Brit. Lib. ADD MS 57,962.
[25] Motion, Andrew, *The Lamberts* (Chatto & Windus 1986), p. 165-6.
[26] Warlock, Peter, *Frederick Delius* (Bodley 1923), p. 130.

3. Suicide, Accident or—Murder?

It is not my intention here to pursue the matter of Philip Heseltine's death at length. He was found dead in a gas-filled basement room in Tite Street, Chelsea, on 17 December 1930. The Coroner told the jury to decide whether the death was accidental or intentional,[1] but they were unable to say.

Tite Street, Chelsea
Plaque unveiled, 10 December 1984.

I recall that after the Peter Warlock Society had been founded by Pat Mills thirty years ago, we amicably divided, on reading the open verdict, into two camps: 'suicide' and 'accident'. Little did we think of a third possibility. Now the suggestion is presented to us of murder by van Dieren, an expert on poisons (NH p. 80) and chief beneficiary of the will (NH pp. 97, 172) in which he was left 'everything he possessed' (NH p. 31)! Bernard van Dieren (1887-1936) was born in Rotterdam of mixed Dutch and French (Scholes says Irish) blood. He came to London in 1909. 'The family trait,' says Denis ApIvor,[2] was bankruptcy, which affected both his father and his mother . . . and, later, his son.' Also from 1912, he became a chronic invalid. He 'resolutely refused,' continues ApIvor, 'to admit the possibility of Heseltine's suicide'. After van Dieren's death, the widow was intensely sensitive about his dependence on Heseltine who was 'handing over sums of money and devoting all his posthumous royalties to van Dieren, though he had a son of his own.'

Van Dieren himself had a son who shared not only his name, Bernard J. van Dieren (Junior) but also his proclivity for insolvency and borrowing. The latter involved, amongst others, Arthur Bliss and Adrian Boult, who never had their money back. After a spell as a fund-raiser, collaborating with the son-in-law of Dr. Thomas Jones C.H. (a powerful figure behind Lloyd George and also for the appointment to the Gregynog Chair of Music of Walford Davies), B. J. van D. (Junior) 'managed' the funds of the Elgar Birthplace Trust, narrowly avoiding prosecution, and also of the Peter Warlock Society,[3] including a disastrously expensive concert in 1968.

A photograph of Philip's will is shown before page 89 of the son's new memoir, in which he bequeathed 'all my real and personal property whatsoever and wheresoever' to Bernard van Dieren. At least this tends to vindicate those of us who were on the side of 'accident'—he had so much work on hand to live for at the time—and van Dieren had admitted that he and his wife were the last persons to see Philip alive (NH p. 172). Can it be supposed that Philip may at last have refused to lend any more money to a persistent sponger? I suggest this, since Philip, according to E. J. Moeran, in the last few years of his life, became less of a disciple of van

The van Dierens, father and son.

By courtesy of Raymond Monk.

Dieren than Gray and 'more independent'.[4] There would be
a motive then, with many well-to-do characters in the
background, as in an Agatha Christie who-dunnit.

Nor can we overlook the fact that, four years previously,
Philip's book on Gesualdo, *Musician & Murderer*[5] had been
published. What a macabre prediction!—or coincidence?

A further, fourth, possibility has more recently been put
forward: that of a fake suicide which went wrong. The reader
is referred to John Mitchell's article, 'Suicide, Accident,
Murder . . . or Maybe Something Else?' of 1993.[6] It was not
possible for many years to see the official transcript of the
inquest, so we have had to rely on Gray's account of it. Now,
I understand, it has been made available to Barry Smith.[7]

When the 'great master' Schubert died on 19th November 1828 at the even younger age of 31 (with vastly more composition to show for it than Warlock, even though the latter produced a prodigious amount of editing and literary work as well, as Fred Tomlinson's statistics point out.[8]), his last feverish creations included the highly inspired song, *Der Doppelgänger,* in which Heine and he together take the listener across to the other side of the great death divide (he had, of course, done this before in *Erlkönig*).

Warlock, just a hundred years later, with poet Bruce Blunt, goes similarly in his final months to the vast world of 'beyond' in *The Frostbound Wood* (written in November 1929) and in *The Fox* ('conceived and completed, words and music, within 18 hours' in July 1930[9] and sung shortly afterwards by the distinguished tenor, Parry Jones). Later, scored by van Dieren, it was performed at a first memorial concert in London on 23rd February 1931, two months after the composer's death. Next year, three songs, including *The Fox,* were performed by William R. Allen of Dolgellau in a concert at Gregynog Hall, only eight miles from his mother's home (see programme on p. 55).

Significantly, the first of these two last songs, *The Frostbound Wood,* shows Philip's mother's religious world. 'Mary that was the Child's mother Met me in the frostbound wood'. It may also owe something to Aleister Crowley (see below), who in 1899 had written a Hymn to Isis and then 'found favour with the Vatican' by changing Isis to Mary. The second, described by Constant Lambert as Warlock's *Doppelgänger,* starts with a ghostly hunting call, at 'The Fox Inn', and gives a stark and deathly picture of his step-father's country pursuits. 'High on the wall Above the cask Laughs at you all The fox's mask . . . The crumbled hoof, The hounds of dust . . . You will not call, I shall not stir When the fangs fall From that brown fur'. Thus both songs impinge on the domestic scene in mid-Wales. Gray went so far, in contemplating these songs, as to suggest that the composer was a reincarnation of

37

Beddoes[10] and they do certainly seem to support his suicide hypothesis by their depressive sadness.

Philip made one of his rare chamber music settings of Beddoes in 1926. *Sorrow's Lullaby* is for soprano, baritone (so-called) and string quartet and Dr. Copley finds it still influenced by van Dieren at this late stage.[11] It is not entirely characteristic. Bernard van Dieren, reputed to have made at least one ghostly appearance after his death in 1936, was said by Constant Lambert to have 'dictated' the palindrome in his ballet, *Horoscope,* in 1937.[12] There is a theory, incidentally, that the bits that wear thin in Lambert's brilliant book, *Music Ho!,* came from Gray and Philip (see Motion, Andrew, *The Lamberts,* Chatto, 1986, p. 202, who also, with no justification, states that Philip gassed himself). The Radio 3 Friday Play, 'Music & Murder', of 15th June 1990, based on Philip's Gesualdo book is, of course, fiction.

The play, *Poison Pen,* by Ronald Harwood, with Tom Courtenay as star, was put on at the Royal Exchange Theatre, Manchester, in May 1993. Ostensibly this is based on the personality of Peter Warlock, but it demonstrates well how forcibly Cecil Gray's interpretation of events has made its mark on later writers. Both main ideas represented, that of a split personality and the assumption of suicide, are now considered less likely to be true. According to one review[13] the composer also fluctuated between a 'dancer toyboy and a mysogynous affair with a neurotic floosie', while another[14] asks, 'Did Heseltine really keep a male lover in London and a neurotic female music student in the country?' And was plagiarism such an obsession as it is made out? This play shows how easily false notions can come to be accepted as fact and how fiction can lead to more fiction! The only word which may be said to ring true in this play is the 'Poison' in its title.

As long ago as 1954 Harry T. Moore[15] had gratuitously told us that Philip escaped from some amatory difficulties by turning on the gas, thus embellishing further the suicide theory.

Van Dieren appears to have exerted a 'baneful' influence not only on Lambert but on others.[16] That is the opinion of Richard Shead, biographer of Constant Lambert. It seems to be diametrically opposed to that of Eiluned Davies, who writes than van Dieren and Philip 'had a stimulating and benign influence on one another's work'.[17]

The two views are neatly summarised by Lewis Foreman, who concludes that many of van Dieren's admirers 'came to grief at a comparatively early age'.[18]

Although I cannot now share her great enthusiasm for van Dieren as a composer, it must be conceded that Miss Davies is doing much to keep his name alive by her recordings. These include Ronald Stevenson's transcription for piano of his *String Quartet No. 5,* a work (one of six quartets) originally for the unwieldy combination of two violins, cello and doublebass.

In 1983 and 1985 van Dieren's complete piano works were recorded by Eiluned Davies for the British Music Society on two audio cassettes (BMS 402 and BMS 405). Many had not been previously recorded. Miss Davies was a pupil of Frida Kindler, the wife of the composer, who herself had studied with Busoni. The last piano piece of 1934, composed as a birthday gift for Frida, was called *Piccolo Pralinudettino Fridato* (on a CD: BML001, 1992). The title was in the eccentric tradition which had earlier influenced Philip, whose song, *Arthur O'Bower* from *Candlelight,* written in Wales in 1923, was marked 'Tumultuosissimamente'.

Lambert dedicated his *Piano Concerto,* 1931, to Philip's memory—a very different work in its 25 minutes to Sorabji's 176 pages. By the time he had finished writing 'Mi Contra Fa',[19] Sorabji, previously a friendly critic, had obviously lost interest in Philip and his music. He was still of the opinion that van Dieren was some sort of a superhuman giant on a par with the great Italian painters and even to be compared with an El Greco saint. He thought also that Cecil Gray was at least a composer of note, but poor Philip is left only with the comment that inspiration was like a fly in treacle.

How wrong can you be and how easy it is for us to be wise after the event!

If Philip became suicidal because of the neglect of his compositions, can we be too surprised? This angle is expressed by E. J. Moeran in a letter to Arnold Dowbiggin of 18 February 1931.[20] 'The majority of his songs,' he wrote, 'he never even heard sung. I cannot help feeling that he might have been still with us had he been given some of the recognition he deserved.' Moeran, however, did not say that Philip was often his own worst enemy in this respect (as will be seen below), treading frequently on the corns of those who might well have promoted performances.

The argument of those opposed to the suicide theory was that Philip had a considerable amount of creative work in hand and unfinished. This is reinforced by the picture of him as fit and cheerful in his last months. 'Shortly before his death . . . he called at my house in Oxford,' wrote Sir Richard Terry, 'healthy, tanned and exuberantly high-spirited . . . exultant with the joy of life.'[21]

On this evidence there is no need, of course, to accept the murder hypothesis, which is refuted with medical expertise by Denis ApIvor (who knew van Dieren well) in a letter to the *Peter Warlock Society Newsletter,* No. 47 of September/October 1991.

There is, however, plenty of food for thought.

Many conflicting views have accumulated, mostly based on the assumption that the witnesses at the inquest, as well as Cecil Gray, were reliable. Certain assumptions have grown up over the years and 'What is asserted by critics becomes, through repetition, an orthodoxy.'[22] One is that Philip 'put the cat out'—but no-one saw him do it; the cat was seen outside in the yard the next morning. Was the gas tap faulty or not and was the door locked on the inside or the outside?

The woman who had lived in the flat, Barbara Peache, had gone out about 8pm, when 'two friends were with him', and didn't return until after the death. Van Dieren, who said he was with Philip from 10.40 until after midnight on the Tuesday, said they had been out for a drink at 'The Duke of Wellington' during the evening, although the post-mortem subsequently may well have shown no sign of alcohol in the body. Philip's voice was heard in a lit-up flat early on the Wednesday, when he is thought to have bolted the door from the inside. So, if we accept the murder hypothesis, it would make it seem difficult for the murderer to get out. But there remains the possibility of van Dieren administering slow-acting poison earlier. It is also worth giving a thought to the idea that van Dieren, who according to Nigel was a frequenter of satanists, could have wielded considerable powers of suggestion. Philip was always ready to do what a strong personality proposed. Was there, perhaps, a homosexual or a drugs connection? And would this have led to his taking his own life?

A curiosity is that, according to Gray, the policeman who was called to the flat rather later, found a draft will starting with 'This is the last will of me, Peter Warlock, 12A Tite St', whereas Nigel reproduces an official will starting with 'This is the last Will and Testament of me Philip Arnold Heseltine of Cefn Bryntalch Abermule Montgomeryshire' (which goes on to revoke all previous testamentary dispositions). So, after constantly supporting the publication of van Dieren's music rather than his own,[23] was he trying at the last minute to free himself from a satanic influence, assert himself and cut van Dieren out of his will?

---

[1] Gray, *op.cit.*, p. 295.
[2] ApIvor, Denis, 'Bernard van Dieren', *The Music Review*, Vol. 47, No. 4, November 1986/7.
[3] See Parrott, Ian, 'Elgar & Peter Warlock', *The Elgar Society Journal*, May, 1994.

[4] Cockshott, Gerald, 'E. J. Moeran's Recollections of Peter Warlock' in *The Musical Times,* March 1955.

[5] Heseltine, P. with Gray, Cecil, *Carlo Gesualdo, Musician & Murderer* (Kegan Paul 1926).

[6] Mitchell, John, *Peter Warlock Society Newsletter* No. 50, April 1993, p. 14.

[7] Smith, Barry, *Peter Warlock: The Life of Philip Heseltine (1894-1930),* (OUP 1994).

[8] Tomlinson, *op.cit.,* Vol. I, p. 45.

[9] Copley, *The Music of Peter Warlock,* p. 143.

[10] Gray, *op.cit.,* p. 302.

[11] Copley, *op.cit.,* pp. 44, 175.

[12] Shead, Richard, *Constant Lambert* (1973, Rev. Thames 1987), p. 112.

[13] Thornber, Robin, *The Guardian,* 17th May 1993.

[14] Spencer, Charles, *Daily Telegraph,* 17th May 1993.

[15] Moore, Harry T., *The Priest of Love. A Life of D. H. Lawrence* (Heinemann, 1954, rev. 1974).

[16] Shead, *op.cit.,* p. 28.

[17] Letter to the author of 28 July 1993.

[18] Foreman, Lewis, *From Parry to Britten, British Music in Letters, 1900-1945* (Batsford 1987).

[19] Sorabji, K. S., *Mi Contra Fa. The Immoralisings of a Machiavellian Musician* (Porcupine Press 1947), p. 149.

[20] Self, Geoffrey, *The Music of E. J. Moeran* (Toccata 1986), p. 74.

[21] Gray, *op.cit.,* p. 273.

[22] Malcolm Noel, 'Tarnishing the Iron Lady', about Margaret Thatcher and politics, but relevant (*Daily Telegraph,* 21 October 1993).

[23] Tomlinson, Fred, *Warlock and van Dieren* (Thames 1978), p. 36.

4. Psychology and Magic

Let us dwell now on the psychology of Philip Heseltine, an essentially weak character, not the hero of a 'Great Composers' album, where the lives were supposed to be as excellent as the compositions, but a timid and withdrawn loner, tied to his mother both by apron and by purse strings. I have known a man (who was a full no-nonsense homosexual) who had both a dominating mother and a tiny handwriting—and he loved Elizabethan music and risqué jokes. This similarity to Heseltine may of course be coincidental, but it seems that there must always be varying degrees of maternal effect. The five Warlock songs called *Lillygay,* composed at Cefn-Bryntalch, July to August 1922, are amongst his finest and the majority of the Neuburg verses chosen by the composer give a 'female bias'. [1]

Most of Philip's songs are dedicated, if at all, to men, including the beautiful *Cradle Song* of 1927 (to Alec Rowley), this particular text looking rather like something for a woman to sing.

Elgar, too, was more influenced by his mother than by his father. Elgar's wife, moreover, took over as mother-figure, helping him to the absolute top of the conventional ladder of respectability. The feminist effect may have been slight but he showed—like Philip (see below)—a comparative lack of affection towards his one offspring; and he shared a somewhat immature friendship with men more than with women. With Elgar it meant juvenile 'japes' and with Peter Warlock braggart drinking bouts. A striking difference, however, is that Philip, from a well-to-do background, lived as if he was always short of money (which he was), whereas Elgar, from a poor background, enjoyed living like a lord (which he did when he could).

Philip always wanted to change his circumstances. Even the name 'Warlock' is an escape from the real world—a male witch, who practices sorcery, i.e. who uses supernatural powers. He first wrote under this pseudonym in 1916.[2]

Philip, having joined the *avant-garde* set (NH p. 75) at the Café Royal in 1914, came immediately under the influence of Aleister Crowley, who became one of his 'masters' (NH p. 85). 'Magic was to be a ruling influence that succeeded motor-bicycles. . . .' (he had been a tear-about motor-bike fanatic) 'and Satan never let him go' (NH p. 76). Crowley at that time had 'a considerable following' (NH p. 84), the aim being to gain 'power over people and over matter'. What, therefore, was more natural than that Philip should seize on this apparent short-cut which would make him master of the environment he desired (NH p. 85), but 'whatever Crowley promised him through his Satanic practices, he had not found it' (NH p. 148) by 1921, when he came across the verses of Victor Neuberg, unless it be in the sheer inspiration of his songs of this period. Indeed, the compositions of the 'Welsh' period, 1921-24, show a marked rise in quantity and excellence. The reader must decide whether there was any new magic in them.

It seems a pity that Philip did not fall under the spell of the enlightened occultism of Cyril Scott.[3] His almost exclusively keyboard style of writing (for hands with a large stretch) owes much to that much under-rated composer,[4] who was also a most original philosopher. Philip's ill-considered assessment in 1917[5] of Scott as an amalgam of Barnby and Wilde is so wide of the mark as to be 'sour grapes'. With *Lotus Land,* 1905, and *Danse Nègre,* 1908, Scott had produced two best sellers; and Philip was not to know that Scott would out-live him by forty years, producing much vigorous, forward-looking music. If Dr. Copley could call *Along the Stream* of 1917 'almost pure van Dieren', may I suggest that the 1922 setting of *In an Arbour Green* is harmonically 'adulterated Scott', with thick chords. (A chord in bar 5 is harder to play in the version transposed down into F too, but that is not the composer's fault). The memorably lilting rhythm in the interludes of *The First Mercy*, 1927, moreover, comes from Scott's *Cuckoo-call*, 1907, and the dropping fourth over dominant and tonic bass from his song, *Prelude*, 1909. That said, it must be added that the Warlock is a very superior product.

Victor Neuburg, 1923.

Picture supplied by Mandrake (Oxford).

45

PETER WARLOCK

Songs with
pianoforte accompaniment

Take, O take those lips away
E min. (b-f♯), F♯ min.

Bayley berith the bell away
E♭ (g-e♭), G

My goſtly fader
E (c-d♯), G

The countryman
A♭ (e♭-a♭)

Mourn no moe
C (a-f), E♭

Whenas the rye
F (b♭-e), G

Sweet content
G (d-g)

Lullaby
D min. (a-d), F min.

There is a lady sweet and kind
B♭ (b♭-f), D♭

My little sweet darling
E (g♯-e), G

The toper's song
G (b-e)

One more river
F (c-f)

As ever I saw
D♭ (d♭-g♭), E♭

Love for love
E (b-e), G

Walking the woods
F (c-f)

The firſt mercy
D min. (f-f)

Noël
C (g-a)

Two shillings each

WINTHROP ROGERS.LTD.
Sole Agents:Hawkes & Son.(London)Ltd
THE BOSTON MUSIC CO., BOSTON, U.S.A.

Title page with Magus, 1918.

It was, instead, to the dark occultism of Aleister (Edward Alexander) Crowley (1875-1947) that Philip was drawn. In *The Confessions of Aleister Crowley,* this most notorious magician, satanist and drug cultist is presented as poet, painter, writer, master chess player, lecher, drug addict and magician.[6] Crowley was 'one of the many who rebelled against the self-righteous, rosy view of society and of men which was held by the Victorians'.[7] Believing he had incarnated many times, he allied himself by the age of 11 to the 'enemies of heaven'. Somerset Maugham's early novel, *The Magician* of 1908, used Crowley as a model of 'a fake, but not entirely a fake'. Philip, also a young rebel against orthodox religion, fell in readily with the mixture of Eastern and Western magic; and must surely have been influenced as well by the sexual promiscuity and deviousness. Even so, Philip, in 1918, 'confessed' in his 15th-century setting, *My Gostly Fader,* rather pointedly, 'First to God, and then to you' (the confessor). So did he have hidden feelings, maybe, of regret or remorse or other conflicting emotions? Whatever it was, it could, as so often with a creative artist, produce some memorable music.

Crowley's father, of Celtic descent, was a strange combination of brewer and Plymouth Brother. Edward Alexander was born in Leamington on 12th October 1875, the year in which Mme. Blavatsky founded the Theosophical Society. The name Aleister was adopted when he was 20. Having left Cambridge without a degree—a foretaste of Philip at Oxford —and, after climbing mountains in Mexico in 1901 and in the Himalayas in 1905, Crowley preferred to work his way up in the Rosicrucian order of the Great White Brotherhood. Reacting, as Philip was to do against his mother's religion, but with St. Augustine's doctrine of 'Love and do what thou wilt', he became a Magus (Initiate) and then in 1921 an Ipsissimus. Magus, of course, is a 'wise man' or wizard and my Latin dictionary suggests Ipsissimus is 'superlative self'.[8] Crowley was fascinated by 'Revelation', becoming known as The Beast 666 (666 means the Sun's energy). Another of

47

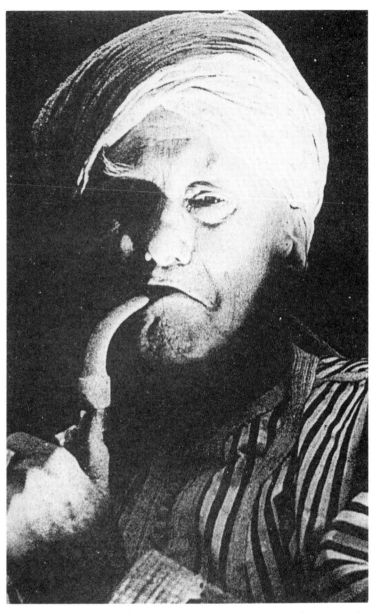

The Arabian alchemist: Crowley smoking his favourite mixture, perique soaked in rum.

'The Confessions of Aleister Crowley' 1970.

those people whose extravagant way of life had involved borrowing money and leaving bad debts, Crowley was also supplied with funds by Neuburg.[9]

Victor Benjamin Neuburg, of a wealthy Jewish family (1883-1940), both agnostic and mystic, was at Trinity College, Cambridge, having founded a Pan Society, when Crowley got hold of him. Pan to Crowley was the Antichrist, symbol of lust and magic, and as the one was looking for pupils, the other for a Master, Crowley had no difficulty in making him into a 'chela' (the pupil of a guru). Crowley later maintained that it was his magic and his willpower which changed Neuburg's writings of 'feeble undergraduate verses' into the production of 'some of the most passionate, intense, musical and lofty lyrics in the language' and when Neuburg left him in 1919, his latest work became 'as lifeless and limp as it was before I took hold'.[10] Described by Crowley as ugly with thick lips, and clumsy with women, this was the subservient and despised Victor Neuburg with his cackling laugh and shambling gait, who then formed a friendship with Philip. This friendship was maintained, so it seems, throughout the 20s, Philip staying with him in August 1923.

It was at Boleskine, near Loch Ness, in June 1909, that Neuburg had already had words 'come to him' which seemed to be a translation of an unknown language. . . and he became entranced.[11] That, of course, was not in the Lowlands. In 1920, however, in Lowland dialect, 'the lines kept coming into his head'.[12] Interesting also is the fact that he was 'going through an Elizabethan period', wearing leggings and breeches and reading Donne.

Neuburg married Kathleen Rose Goddard in Hammersmith in November 1921, and they moved to Vine Cottage, Steyning, Sussex.

The song, *Milkmaids,* of January 1923, comes from an anthology, *Larkspur,* published by the Vine Press, Steyning (which included Neuburg's lyric *Trollie Lollie,* later set by Quilter, 'long after the great years' says Trevor Hold). It had

49

previously brought out *Lillygay,* but Neuburg's name does not appear—nor, for that matter, did it appear in the original edition of the *Lillygay* songs either. Philip did not escape from Crowley, as Neuburg had done, by settling down out of sight in rural Sussex, but remained in his thrall to a considerable degree. He translated Jacobsen on 'The God Pan' for Delius's *An Arabesk* for performance in 1920 in Newport. For Delius, lover of Yorkshire moors and Norwegian mountains, the demonic Pan also personified human passion and transient bliss. Tragically he paid for his *affaires* with his health and by 1922 was confined to a wheelchair. 'For the roads are unending and there is no place to my mind,' cries Yeats, another mystic who was having a profound impact, having already impressed Elgar with his *Grania and Diarmid* in 1901.[13] Yeats and Algernon Blackwood, pantheist friend of Elgar, were both involved to some extent with the Rosicrucians (see Fuller, Jean Overton).

It was to Neuburg that Philip turned after completing the final version of his masterpiece, *The Curlew,* in 1922. We have already noted the 'female bias' in most of the verses chosen by him for the song cycle, *Lillygay.* Jean Overton Fuller writes of 'the magical dilemma' faced by Neuburg[14] who, to her, was not ugly but had 'aristocratic Jewish features'. She does, however, confirm his 'high-pitched cackle' and 'light tenor voice' and was told that his relationship with Crowley was homosexual. He, too, was 'in rebellion against the stuffiness of his family' and was initiated into the Rosicrucian Order of Golden Dawn by Crowley in 1908. 'The male magician [Magus],' said Crowley, must, without losing his virility, cultivate his female side'.[15] Ideally, of course, a wise person, or Magus, should understand both male and female viewpoints, but it may be doubted whether Neuburg, let alone Philip, achieved anything along this road.

Three out of the five verses used in *Lillygay* turn out to be in Lalans (Lowland Scottish dialect English) and the first in English. The fifth poem, 'Rantum Tantum', is not in dialect and it looks as if the less-inspired words have produced the least interesting setting from Philip. The Scottish poet, C. R. Cammell, said Neuburg's ballads were *not* copied.[16] They were his own. It seems here that Philip, like the spirit-possessed Neuburg, was under the (non-Satanic) influence of Crowley. He dedicated the set to a cousin by marriage, Irene Heseltine, but with what result is not known. The songs were first printed in Austria at 'Covie's' expense (see Fred Tomlinson's sleeve-note to Ruth Golden's record, 'My Own Country', 1992). It appears that four out of five of the *Folk Song Preludes* (1917-22) for piano similarly are based on Scottish tunes, so his mind must have roved again to the Celtic country with which he was least familiar.

The influence here must have been of his close friend, Cecil Gray, who had given Lawrence and his wife some Hebridean music 'of which he had made a professional study'.[17] His enthusiasm for the Scottish, moreover, is expressed in a letter to Philip of 3rd January 1922[18] in which he picks out from the second volume of Marjorie Kennedy-Fraser's *Hebridean Songs* one which he describes as one of the most perfect tunes ever written. It is pentatonic, like those already used by Philip.

My friend, Dr. Daniel Jones (7th December 1912-23rd April 1993), a composer of considerable subtlety whose rhythmic experiments may be traced back to the *Sonata* for unaccompanied kettledrums of 1936, told me in a letter of 18th March, a month before his death, that through a mutual friend he was taken to Steyning. They spent the afternoon in the garden behind the charming cottage.

Neuburg had been inviting readers of the *Sunday Referee* to send in poems for possible printing with his comments, so Daniel Jones drew this to the attention of his Swansea friend, Dylan Thomas, 1914-53. Thus, on 3rd September 1933, the great poet had his first *Sunday Referee* poem published, 'That sanity be kept'.[19] Having published Dylan Thomas's first book as the second of the *Sunday Referee* poets (the first being Pamela Hansford Johnson) with the title, *Eighteen Poems*

(December 1934), it could be said that Victor Neuburg 'launched' him.

Here is an example of Neuburg's dream-initiated poetry of 1934, with a sort of old Celtic alliteration. [20]

> Weighed in the Libra-mart, the warlock weighed
> His vision with his voice, triumph with trade.

Apart from its apparent reference to Philip four years after his death, it seems also to foreshadow Dylan Thomas, from whom words would tumble in similar profusion. When asked how he wrote such intricate verse, Dylan at the age of 18 replied, 'Oh, you know, it just seems to flow'. [21]

Philip was also getting Delius out of his system—his book on Delius was written—and he was getting well dug into Elizabethan music.

Delius was a strong and ruthless personality (NH p. 72) and 'Delius's music was literally a blind-alley', writes the son (NH p. 78) but in 'lute and madrigal he found his ability to create something original.' He was *not* dominated by Dr. Fellowes, whose editions of English Lutenists had appeared, or by other 'antiquarians'. Philip's mother, however, remained with her 'conventional' views, 'eternally disapproving' (NH p. 168).

Little has been written so far on the period 1921-24 which Philip spent in mid-Wales surrounded by a family, whose interests diverged so strongly from his own.

 Collins, Brian, 'Warlock & the Lillygay Texts', *Peter Warlock Society Newsletter,* No. 39, July 1987.

[2] Copley, *op.cit.,* p. 11 *et seq.*

[3] Scott, Cyril, *An Outline of Modern Occultism* (Routledge & Kegan Paul, enlarged edn. 1950) and *The Greater Awareness* (Routledge & Kegan Paul 1936 and paperback 1981).

[4] Parrott, Ian, *Cyril Scott & His Piano Music* (Thames 1992), p. 23.

[5] Heseltine, P. in 'The New Age: Scriabin & Cyril Scott', *The Condition of Music in England,* 14 June 1917, pp. 154-6.

[6] Symonds, John and Grant, Kenneth, Eds., *The Confessions of Aleister Crowley* (Hill & Wang, New York, 1970).

[7] Symonds, John, *The Great Beast. The Life & Magick of Aleister Crowley* (Mayflower 1973).

[8] 'Peter Warlock's' earliest songs, published under this pseudonym by Winthrop Rogers from 1918, had a woodcut of a Magus on the title page (see p. 46).

[9] Symonds, *op.cit.,* p. 258.

[10] Symonds, John and Grant, Kenneth, Eds., *op.cit.,* pp. 689, 972.

[11] Fuller, Jean Overton, *The Magical Dilemma of Victor Neuburg* (W. H. Allen 1965), p. 24.

[12] *Ibid.,* p. 203.

[13] See Young, Percy M., 'Elgar & the Irish Dramatists' in *Edward Elgar: Music & Literature,* ed. Raymond Monk (Scolar Press 1993).

[14] Fuller, *ibid.,* pp. 4, 34, 94.

[15] Fuller, *ibid.,* pp. 119, 120.

[16] Fuller, *ibid.,* p. 210.

[17] Moore, Harry T., *op.cit.,* p. 280.

[18] Brit. Lib. ADD MS 57,962.

[19] See Jones, Daniel, ed., *Dylan Thomas: The Poems* (Dent 1971), p. 96. The poem is slightly modified. See also Jones, Daniel, *My Friend Dylan Thomas* (Dent 1977), note on p. 69.

[20] Fuller, *op.cit.,* p. 38.

[21] *Ibid.,* p. 230.

5. Respectable Society

Upper-crust Welsh landed gentry in the nineteenth century tended to be 'anglicised'. Hence the addition of redundant letters, Glyn becoming Glynne and, in the present case, Williams becoming Williames, etc. There was also a tendency to mispronounce and clip words in speaking. Nigel grew up in this atmosphere and, having produced English versions of the poems of Dafydd ap Gwilym in 1944, he contributed to a malicious volume, *Tales of the Squirearchy* in 1946, dealing with the gentry of mid-Wales. One of the great figures of nineteenth-century mid-Wales was David Davies, a top sawyer who went on to making money out of the South Wales coalfields. He was a self-made man from neighbouring Llandinam, who said in 1865, 'I am a great admirer of the old Welsh language . . . Still, I have seen enough of the world to know that the best medium to make money by is the English language.'

On page 118 of his book Nigel mentions several of the landed families. Many of them have left their mark, the Blayneys, for example, at the mansion, Gregynog. Some came in from over the border and bought estates. One of the Dugdales, from Llanfyllin, married into the family of David Davies, 'top sawyer', of Llandinam. Eldrydd Dugdale, by marrying his great-grandson, became the second Lady Davies. The second Lord Davies, who was also an amateur composer who wrote cello sonatas for his wife, was, with his two aunts, Gwendoline and Margaret Davies, to be associated with Gregynog. The aunts lived there throughout the twenties and produced, with their advisers, beautiful books and bindings, a collection of mainly Impressionist paintings, and a series of annual music festivals. Thanks to their music adviser, Sir Walford Davies, eminent performers and the composers, Holst, Vaughan Williams and Elgar were regular visitors.[1] Elgar, in particular, had been entertained at

Gregynog after an indifferent performance of *The Apostles* in Harlech and after a performance, which he enjoyed, of his *Cello Concerto* by Arthur Williams in Aberystwyth in 1924, when he wrote to thank the soloist.[2]

Barbara Dugdale (a sister of Eldrydd, who became the second Lady Davies) married Peter Lewis (1908-1992) of Milford Hall, Newtown, and remembers the tennis parties at Cefn-Bryntalch.

The family of Peter Lewis, like that of Walter, had been concerned with the business of fellmongers and tanners, he being the owner of the artificial lake three miles above Llanidloes, made for the woollen industry.

Philip Heseltine, as we have noted, was honoured only after his death. In the programme of the concert at Gregynog in April 1932, it will be seen that Vaughan Williams was 'Dr.'—he was proud of his earned doctorate—Walford

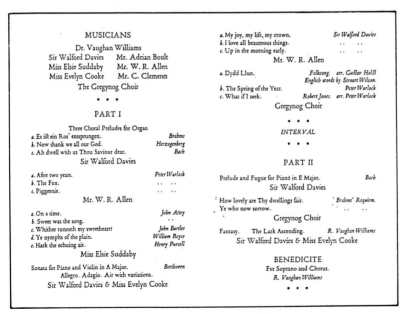

Gregynog, 11 April 1932
A Concert of Vocal and Instrumental Music.
(Gregynog Press printing).

Davies was 'Sir'—he had been knighted in 1926—and 'Mr' Boult was yet to receive his knighthood (in 1937). The following year *My Own Country* and *Sleep* were included.

The Buckley Jones clan did not succeed in the spectacular way of the Davies family who, at Gregynog, were only 8 miles away. Indeed, they lost money, but young Philip reacted against the genteel respectability and also the emphasis on the army, which had led to much tension during the First War, 'when every neighbour had a son or a husband in the Royal Welch Fusiliers or the Welsh Horse' (NH p. 118). However, 'although to everyone he had appeared well enough,' he was exempted from military service with a certificate from a Harley Street doctor (NH p. 119). Even then Philip felt the need to get away. He thought of Delius's Florida orange grove, but the furthest he got was to a remote island off the west coast of Ireland.[3]

He did not believe that peace was worth fighting for,[4] but he longed for personal peace, as he wooed sleep—one of his finest songs is *Sleep* of 1922—knowing that it was unobtainable. The setting of the 16th century John Fletcher's *Sleep* was undertaken as well by Ivor Gurney, 1890-1937,[5] who also died of the effects of gas-poisoning, but in his case as a result of being wounded and gassed in the War.

At the end of the Warlock setting, already marked 'Rather slow', the piano postlude, with increasing dissonance, marked both 'ritenuto molto' and 'diminuendo', gives the perfect impression of a person drifting into the world of sleep. Then, after a pause of silence, the perfect concord, pianissimo, suggests the state of slumber,[6] even though, unlike, say, Haydn, he could not accept a Christian interpretation.

He was to recapture some of the 'going off' effect with Belloc's words at the end of *My Own Country*, 1926:

> When I get to my own country
> I shall lie down and sleep . . .
> And then I shall dream, for ever and all,
> A good dream and deep.

Naturally enough he reacted against the organised religion of his family, so had worshipped the atheistic Delius with his amused sarcasm. We should remember that the bible was read aloud every evening by Walter and 'Covie' in their bedroom (NH p. 93). But here is a paradox. Ironically, some of Warlock's finest works deal with the festivals of the Christian religion, about which he would blaspheme with his friends.

One of his earliest outstanding choral pieces is the haunting *Corpus Christi* of 1919. A setting of a 16th century carol (not Christmas, but a post-Crucifixion lament, with mediaeval imagery) was actually dedicated to the Bishop of Oxford.[7] Three years before this when Philip, although exempt from military service, was anxious about his conscientious objection, Ottoline Morrell had given the Bishop a long lecture on how he should influence the House of Lords in support of the pacifists.[8] So this might well have been in Philip's mind when he decided on the dedication to the Rt. Rev. Thomas B. Strong, who had remembered him as an unconventional undergraduate,[9] when he himself was Dean of Christ Church.

In the devoutly Christian 12th and 13th centuries, the Grail romances were merged with various Irish and Welsh myths, the rituals of the heathen Celtic tradition being integrated with the Eucharist. The wounded knight—'And in that bed there lithe a knight, His woundès bleeding day and night'—is the Anfortas of Celtic legend (Amfortas in Wagner's *Parsifal,* 1882).[10]

Philip here has entered deeply and mystically into the mysterious world of Irish tales and also of the Welsh Mabinogion with its similar stories, which have produced one of his finest compositions. It contrasts starkly with the Lawrence-influenced blasphemous poem, which he sent from Cornwall to Robert Nichols on 16th April 1917, in which Jesus is considered no different from Judas (both vain) and the crucifix should be pulled down.[11] Elgar, in his more

57

reverent way, had made a tragic figure of Judas in *The Apostles* of 1903, and the orchestration for the thirty pieces of silver (score, fig. 171) is infinitely more terrifying than anything Philip would be likely to muster. This is paralleled by Delius's contemptuous assertion that in England music would never be anything until they got rid of Jesus; and Hubert Parry, he once said, would have set the whole bible to music if he'd lived long enough. Even Sorabji noted, however, that the ferociously and fanatically anti-Christian Delius may have feared 'there may be a good deal more [in it] after all than he is willing to admit'.[12] Swayed as he so often was by other rebels' opinions, Philip, as becomes glaringly obvious, wanted to draw attention to himself as well. He must, however, have had feelings of guilt. He cannot entirely have lost his sensitivity to the characters in the Crucifixion story. The text-writer of Delius's *Requiem*[13] he considers 'typical of the worst type of German professor, who might well take lessons in humility from Pontius Pilate'.

Most carols, of course, deal with Christmas, a time celebrated by much beautiful music in Philip's output: *Balulalow*, 1919, later joined (as part of *Three Carols*) to *Tyrley Tyrlow*, 1922 and *Carillon Carilla*, 1929, for example; and *The First Mercy* of 1926, with words by Bruce Blunt,[14] with whom a valuable friendship was first struck up in 1927, both being found 'drunk and disorderly' in February of that year. There is also Philip's only setting of French, the *Chanson du Jour de Noël* of 1925, dedicated to the leading scholar of Tudor church music, Sir Richard Terry, 1856-1938, who contributed a 'tribute' to Gray's biography. Even better is the superb solo version of Bruce Blunt's words, *Bethlehem Down,* made in 1930 from the mixed voices setting of two years earlier. It seems to be the last piece of music he wrote and it is so good that it is difficult to sustain the suicide theory from it.

For some people it was thought rather odd that Philip should write anything to a Cornish text, yet he wrote two Cornish Christmas carols and was very particular about the music being 'inseparably associated' with the words; 'any translation,' he wrote, 'would pervert the whole character of the works.'[15] The first remained in manuscript until after his death. The second, *Can Nadelek* of 1918, found its way into print by 1924. The texts are, of course, reasonably intelligible to those who understand modern Welsh. However, as I have learnt myself with a choir, in No. 2, there are difficulties for Welsh-speaking singers, because the words are so near and yet so far. The Welsh for this title, for example, is *Cân Nadolig.*

The words of *Can Nadelek* are by Henry Jenner. My respected colleague in the Society, Fred Tomlinson, tells us that Philip got the verses for both Cornish carols from the periodical *Celtia.*[16] Some confusion has arisen, however, since Tomlinson has made two people out of Jenner and 'Gwas Myhal'. Copley also is fooled by the use of two names.[17] I am much indebted to my friend, J. E. Caerwyn Williams, for explaining this. Jenner, the author of a Cornish Grammar, worked as a member of staff of the British Museum and wrote poetry in Cornish. 'Gwas Myhal' was in fact his 'poetic' name, which means 'Servant of St. Michael', Myhal being a variant form of Myghal. Similarly The Servant of Patrick is 'Gwas Pedrig', giving the modern Gospatrick. Professor Caerwyn Williams, moreover, sees no reason for not keeping Jenner's spelling: *Can Nadelek* (it is listed, with k and i, as *Kan Nadelik* in Tomlinson, *A Peter Warlock Handbook,* Vol. I, p. 15, and in Copley, *The Music of Peter Warlock, Alphabetical Index,* pp. 316, 317 & 320) since Philip had used these spellings, but the publisher, Winthrop Rogers, used 'c's' and 'ek'. Jenner's material was left to the British Museum (B.M. MS 52905). Patrick Mills, who works in the Music Library of the British Library, tells me that much of this deals with Manx.

Philip had studied Cornish when in Cornwall a second time in 1917, having fallen out with D. H. Lawrence. The language, being extinct, attracted him above all others, as a private language (NH p. 129), though Gray described it as 'preposterous'.[18] Needless to say, he made 'great progress with the Irish language, and was soon speaking and reading it with ease. . .' (NH p. 135), while in Wales, his son, Nigel, was taking his first steps across the dining-room floor. Still interested in a pan-Celtic movement and comparative Celtic philology, his attention moved also to Breton. This involved becoming friendly with Paul Ladmirault, 1877-1944, a composer and collector of the folk-songs of Brittany, who has the distinction and good fortune of being the dedicatee of Philip's most popular and widely-known composition in all its versions, *Capriol*, based on Arbeau dance tunes.[19]

When Dr. Daniel Jones was completing his research for his M.A. (before 1939), he was unable, he said, to find Thoinot Arbeau's *Orchésographie* in the British Museum. So where, before 1926, did Philip find it? My first reaction was to suppose that his friend, Ladmirault, found it for him in the Bibliothèque Nationale in Paris. However, Patrick Mills thinks that the 1588 edition can have been missing for only a short period. There are now, he says, three copies, the second of which was to replace the first—which was subsequently found. Alternatively, after seeing it in 1925, when Cyril Beaumont made a translation, Philip may have 'pinched' the first copy!

There is no evidence that Philip wished to complete his Celtic knowledge by the serious study of Manx, but we shall see that he was deeply conscious of the language on his doorstep: Welsh.

He loved Wales and the Welsh language, as his unpublished letters to Cecil Gray in the most artistically productive year, 1922, show,[20] but his mother and her friends were 'anglicised' and mostly unaware.

The scene is well painted in a letter to me of 1964 from Mrs. Betty Crawshaw, a member of the Banner family, who had bought an estate nearby at Caerhowel. Both Col. Crewe-Read (see below) and Capt. Humphries had been amused when the bearded Philip was seen carrying his own beer-mug two miles down the cefn (ridge) to the 'local' at Llandyssil (the Upper House Inn) or to an inn near Montgomery station. A beard was, of course, unorthodox for a respectable young man in the twenties. He walked very fast and they heard him humming and whistling in the lane. This Capt. Humphreys will have been Charles Martin Strick Humphreys, then of Garthmyl Hall, whose ancestor, Charles Humphreys, 1770-1804, sold part of his Pennant Estate in 1800 to Pryce Buckley Williames (see above p. 20) of Glanhafren, Abermule, for £7,500.[21] His daughter, Stella, in 1922, became one of the first lady magistrates in the county,[22] becoming later the first lady High Sheriff in the whole country since Elizabethan times. The family was also related to Judge Christmas Humphreys, who died in 1983, eminent Q.C. and a rare Western exponent of Buddhism.

'Covie,' said Mrs. Crawshaw, 'was sweet and kind' and after Philip's death she gently cried to herself 'around the house with the door to the piano room open' so that she could hear Betty singing some of his songs. It was 'very distressing indeed,' and it seems that 'Covie' could not always tell which were his songs and which were not.

More recently I have heard from Mrs. Ann Crichton (née Montgomery), who remembers Walter and 'Covie' (who used rouge) as the kindest of old couples.

Mrs. J. D. K. Williams (née Prudence Trevor) says, 'Aunt Covie was warm, friendly and altogether loveable and wonderful with children. She had a ladies maid . . . (but) her standard of living was somewhat higher than their income justified. I never remember meeting the composer—he was always a shadowy figure that was mentioned in awe—but I remember meeting his wife ['Puma'], who moved with a slinky feline grace and quite obviously was not of the same order of society as we were.' This ties up with Nigel's description: a 'complete absence of acceptable background . . . to the stayed, bodiced and corseted women of the time'

The Piano Room.

(NH p. 107 *et seq*). As a young girl, Mrs. Riba Dugdale, now of Kerry, found 'Mrs. Covie' a somewhat alarming figure, since she was always dressed totally in black. Although she never met either Philip or Nigel, Mrs. Dugdale remembers feeling 'very smart' when she could tell her friends that the composer of *Adam Lay Ybounden* lived near. She sang this carol at school, her copy then costing 3d!

Another family living near was of the Crewe-Reads of Pennant, across the river Severn and within sight of Cefn-Bryntalch (NH p. 118). I am indebted to Mrs. Joan Orr, a member of that distinguished family, for her observations on Nigel and his father from the time they settled there, she being a year older than Nigel, her mother a great friend of 'Covie'.

> As children living a 1920's country life our interests were more sporting than cultural, shooting rabbits, taking turns to ride his Shetland pony, bird nesting and climbing trees. Nigel had violin lessons but at that period had little interest in music. We both attended weekly dancing classes which he hated, though later. . . he did enjoy teen-age dances but always told me that he had no interest in English girls; he must have continued with this view as his first wife was the daughter of White Russians, his second French and his present wife Thai.
>
> When Nigel's father was at Cefn-Bryntalch, I was aware of tension and we children were banished to the attics to play. There seemed little contact between father and son even at this early stage. I remember Nigel saying, 'I wonder how long he is staying?', though he never expressed any dislike. He was nervous of talking to his father whom he really only met at meal times.

Philip himself was not obviously an affectionate father. He once wrote a letter to a publisher declining to write songs for the young, which developed into a diatribe against all children. [23]

While at Shrewsbury, Nigel became interested in the Roman Catholic faith, becoming a convert. His son is being brought up a Catholic. An exact contemporary at school at Shrewsbury (being in the same house) was Brian Inglis, the writer on dreams and the paranormal, who died at the age of 76 on 13th February 1993. He thought that modern man's insistence that we live in a fundamentally material world is not only misconceived but is leading to terrible mistakes. [24]

Nigel, his Thai wife and 10-year-old son were at Mrs. Orr's in the spring of 1992, when he came over from Australia for the launching of his book, which he ends with a sincere prayer for his father's soul: *Requiem aeternam dona eo Domine.* Descended from Thomas de Crewe of the time of Henry III and John Read of Roch Castle, the Crewe-Reads settled in Montgomeryshire in 1870, building the new mansion, Plas Dinam, in 1871. This house at Llandinam passed afterwards to the descendants of David Davies, 'top sawyer'. The present occupants are the third Lord Davies and his family.

[1] Parrott, Ian *The Spiritual Pilgrims* (Christopher Davies, Llandybie 1968).

[2] Parrott, Ian, *op.cit.,* p. 81.

[3] Robert Beckhard, I understand, is writing on this.

[4] Copley, *op.cit.,* p. 7. Letter to Delius of October 1914.

[5] Moore, Gerald, *Singer & Accompanist* (Methuen 1955), p. 95.

[6] Parrott, Ian, 'Music of the Spheres is heard?' in *Two Worlds,* November 1977, p. 297.

[7] See also Aplvor, Denis, *op.cit.,* p. 121.

[8] Seymour, Miranda, *op.cit.,* p. 349.

[9] Copley, The Music of Peter Warlock, *op.cit.,* p. 7.

[10] See Chrétien de Troyes, *Percival: The Story of the Grail,* trans. Nigel Bryant, (Cambridge, 1982). See also, Stone, Alby, *The Bleeding Lance* (Heart of Albion Press, 1992).

[11] Copley, *A Turbulent Friendship,* p. 29.

[12] Sorabji, K. S., *op.cit.,* p. 30.

[13] Warlock, Peter, *Frederick Delius* (Bodley 1923), p. 108.

[14] Tomlinson, Fred, *Warlock & Blunt* (Thames, 1981).

[15] Heseltine, P., Letter to Colin Taylor, 13 June 1918.

[16] Tomlinson, *op.cit.,* Vol. I, p. 31. Note (20). This should not be confused with *'Celtica',* a journal of a much later date.

[17] Copley, *op.cit.,* p. 189.

[18] Gray, C., *op.cit.,* p. 162.

[19] See also Kington, Beryl 'Rowley Rediscovered' (Thames 1993) p. 38.

[20] Quotes from these letters are by courtesy of Robert Beckhard, New York.

[21] Humphreys, C. L. J., 'The Charles Humphreys of Montgomery and Berriew (*Montgomeryshire Collections,* Vol. 70, of 1982).

[22] Lewis, Peter, *Eveline. An Account of Mrs. Hugh Lewis, M.A., J.P.* (Gomer Press, 1986), p. 78.

[23] Mills, Patrick, in *P.W. Society Newsletter* No. 34 (January 1985).

[24] Ruth West, Letter to *Daily Telegraph,* 17th February 1993.

6. Wild Wales

On reading Philip's letters to Cecil Gray we are reminded not only of his enthusiasm and vitality at the age of 28, but also of Gray's insensitivity to the attractions of the Welsh countryside over which Philip was tramping for considerable distances. Early in 1922 Philip went for 'an enormously long walk', skipping up and down Plynlimon (2467 ft),[1] like a two-year-old mountain goat. He then offered Gray a 'short' trek from Dylife, where he admired the falls, to the Anchor, his favourite pub, a total of perhaps 25 miles, not including getting there. With some parts dating back to the 14th century, the Anchor Inn was a resting point on the Shropshire border for drovers with their animals 'on the hoof'. Eight miles (or nine miles across country) south of Philip's home, it is still well preserved. No doubt an attraction was the escape it offered from the 'dry' Welsh Sunday of those days.

At the Anchor Inn.

But in the autumn the hapless Gray was expected to take part in a marathon scramble which started with 8 days from Ludlow to Plynlimon, sleeping rough—and that was only half of it, Ludlow to Knighton, about 15 miles, being merely a start. The clambering over the bleak mountain-sides from Plynlimon on to Dylife would no doubt have been too much in itself. 'The capacity of your noble legs I know,' wrote Philip in the autumn, 'but 27 miles per diem would doubtless prove excessive.'

Elsewhere, after enthusing about Aran Fawddwy (2971 ft), 'which is a real crag with, I believe, some quite exciting rock-ledges thereon,' he rightly assesses his friend's lack of prowess with 'But you will probably have neither time nor inclination for this.'

Indeed, the huge distances and climbs were positively Borrow-like. George Borrow had covered some of the same parts in his *Wild Wales* seventy years before, especially near Machynlleth and the high ground to the East.

Careful pronunciations are given by Philip in his letters, e.g. Cwm Hir (koom heer). After ascending Plynlimon you

Looking towards Dylife from the top of Plynlimon.

'make for Dylife (dŭleevy) along the north side of the lake Bugeilyn (bigāle-ĭn) . . . a stupendous view of the mountains towards the north. At Dylife there is a magnificent waterfall . . . 130 feet high, from an overhanging crag on the edge of a terrific and gloomy gorge which should always be seen towards evening. You then make for Llanbrynmair (-mire) station.'

There actually was a station there in 1922, but Philip was going further north on foot. Borrow, in October 1854, talks of the great chain of Aran as the 'wildest part of Wales' (chapter 54) with 'crags of wondrous forms'. David Davies, 'top sawyer', was not finally to cut through the rocks for the railway line, with its station there, until 1861. How strangely some lines and stations have come and gone. Now, seventy years later, most railway stations, including Llanbrynmair, Abermule and Montgomery, have been extracted by the Beeching axe; and many dams and reservoirs such as Clywedog and Nant-y-moch have been added instead to the landscape.

David Davies became a director of the Cambrian Railways in 1867. At this time, his fortune amassed in South Wales through the Ocean Coal Company gave him the new name of 'Davies the Ocean'. A few years later he built his last and more modest railway line, six-and-a-half miles long and just over the hill from his home at Llandinam. The Van Railway (Van is an Anglicised corruption of Y Fan), was first for lead mines and then in 1873 for passengers. Only second and third class carriages were provided, so there were no seats for the 'gentry'. It ran through the land of Captain Offley Malcolm Crewe-Read, R.N., whose eldest son, Col. Randolph Offley Crewe-Read, D.S.O., J.P., was the father of Mrs. Joan Orr.

In the twenties, the First Lord Davies, grandson of David Davies, would ride along the track, following the hounds. There was little risk of encountering a train as no train was expected more than two or three times a week.[2] He was raised to the peerage as Baron Davies of Llandinam in 1932.

This railway is of special interest to us since Philip wrote an article for *The Locomotive* of 15th January 1912, called 'The Van Railway'. The remains of the station at Caersws can still be seen. The popular Welsh poet Ceiriog (John Hughes) was general manager of this railway. It must, says Wynford Vaughan-Thomas, have been the only railway in the world with a poet as general manager. The passenger traffic never paid but the shareholders got a lot of poetry for their money.[3]

Philip had already shown his interest in a letter sent to his mother, dated 1st May 1904, which is shown in Nigel's biography. The nine-year-old boy had just started at Stone House, a preparatory school at Broadstairs. This letter can be seen now in a new light: 'You will share the kisses and love with Walter at Cefn-Bryntalch, won't you. I hope Lumley will have a pleasant journey. Tell Walter that there is an article on the "Tanat Valley Light Railway" . . .' details and drawing follow. And for good measure he squeezes in Bishop Heber and Southey as visitors, showing his precocious involvement in poetry both spiritual and romantic. But more than anything it opens up, perhaps, the last glimpse of a happy family life before the rift set in.

The railway over which Philip had enthused had in fact been opened only four months before his letter was written. It ran for 14 miles along the valley of the Tanat, leaving the Welshpool-Oswestry line. It closed in December 1960.[4] Walter shared Philip's passion for railways, having a 'phenomenal knowledge of the time-tables of all the railways in Western Europe' (NH p. 93).

If Cecil Gray had accepted the huge round trip (see sketch map), he would have been 'let off' the final 30 miles of the circuit from Abermule back to Ludlow. The uninteresting flat main roads were to have been negotiated by Walter and a car.

Continuing his meticulous pronunciation guides, Philip, in a letter of 14th June 1922, gives Cefn Bryntalch (without its aristocratic hyphen on this occasion) a locally correct sound. Even Welsh speakers do not always agree on the 'y' in such a compound word, but Philip (forgetting to treat the f as v in Cefn) gives 'Brŭntach, the ch being aspirate'. This implies that the y is like the u in gun (as it should be also in Gregynog) and the l may be left out. Even so, polite upper-class neighbours would be more likely to say 'Cevn Brunt'k', clipping the ending much as the South Walians would convert the home of the Lord Lieutenant of Glamorgan from Coedarhydyglyn to 'C'drigl'n'. 'In Wales,' he continues, 'the name of one's house becomes a kind of second surname . . . Mr Jones might be anyone but Mr. Jones-Cefn-Bryntalch is distinctive.'

Philip Heseltine's long walk in 1922.

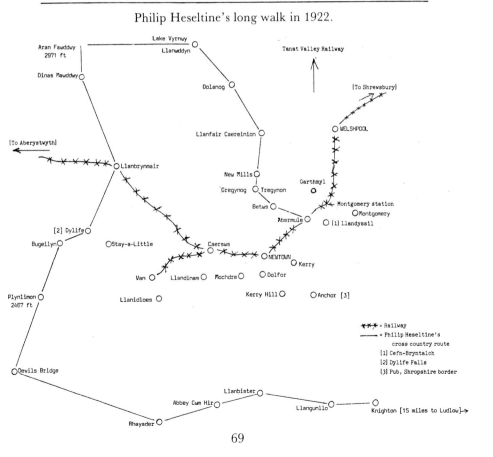

Elgar also loved fantasising with the Welsh language and in a letter to his Welsh friend, Troyte Griffith, on 17th March 1906, he had imagined their respective ancestors, Aelgar, an outlawed Saxon, in alliance with King Gruffydd ab Llywelyn, sacking the city of Hereford.[5]

Reading between the lines of the new book, which does not mention these long solitary tramps except in general terms (NH p. 26), it seems that they were not only an escape from Philip's family but an inspiration. If Gray had actually turned up, the result would probably have been like the out-of-condition Fenby puffing behind the athletic Grainger, as depicted in Ken Russell's superb film on Delius of 1967 called 'A Song of Summer'.

In a letter of 7th September 1922,[6] Gray did politely excuse himself with 'after all I shall not be able to come to Wales this month.' This was despite his offer earlier to bring a 'certain Crowleyian compound', which would certainly have caused a stir in the respectable Buckley Jones household, where even a cheroot had to be puffed outside (NH p. 117).

Philip was now on his feet in open country with sheep tracks. Ten years earlier he had covered the roads from the Cardiganshire coast, through Lampeter, to Whitney and on past Knighton to Gloucestershire by motor-bike, sometimes with a lady passenger in the side-car. If possible, as on 5th June 1913, he would have taken in the 'Anchor' inn on the way.

Starting by trekking more than 15 miles from his home to the slopes of Plynlimon, Philip enjoyed scrambling on over the bleakest, remotest parts of the country to the Dylife falls—still quite a daunting prospect, even with the new Nant-y-moch reservoir to guide one today. He must have been really fit at that time.

The only sound in his ears would have been the various calls of the Welsh curlew, which had already led him to its Irish cousins of W. B. Yeats's poetry:

'O, Curlew, cry no more in the air'

70

Dylife Falls.

Yeats, 1865-1939, deeply interested in the occult and in Celtic mythology, had helped to found the Irish National Theatre Company at the Abbey Theatre, Dublin. Philip met him during his stay in Dublin in 1917 and also contemplated writing an opera on an old Irish tale, 'Liadain and Curither'. As we have seen, Philip gave a lecture, 'What Music Is', at the Abbey Theatre and played some Bartók the next year.[7]

At the end of Philip's significant work, *The Curlew*, the outcome of several years' shaping, the solo voice sings 'I wander by the edge of this desolate lake'. Surely this must have come to mean Bugeilyn to Philip, the furthest point from any human habitation in what is still largely a natural wilderness. It was a serious attempt to escape from the turbulent relationships and Bohemian company of London. But he was between the Devil and the Deep Blue Sea—or perhaps Crowley and the Irish Sea.

'She looked in my heart one day
And saw your image was there'

Returning to mid-Wales, Philip was faced again by his mother's upper-crust way of life and his step-father's

Bugeilyn Lake.

72

Cleft in rock near Bugeilyn, possibly a place for magical Druid ritual, similar to Bryn Celli Ddu in Anglesey.

uncongenial family friends. Crowley in his *Confessions* had said, 'I have always felt with Shelley that parental tyranny is the most indefensible kind.'[8] Philip will have been impressed also by the mountaineering reputation of Crowley, who led the—unsuccessful—Kangchenjunga (28,215 ft) expedition of 1905, up the third highest Himalayan peak in the world (not actually conquered until 1955).

This will have encouraged those long lonely excursions, which in the case of *The Curlew* produced one of his most characteristic compositions, where the opposing influences of Delius and Bartók have been blended together to create what we now know as his highly personal style. Although there are traces of the hard-edged Bartók in the passage, with its rhythmic snap, from bar 9; and although there are traces of the soft-edged Delius at the voice's second entry, 'Pale brows, still hands,'; and although the structure is to some extent cobbled together, *The Curlew* is Warlock's most consistent extended composition. There is nothing else like it, with its tragic melancholy, in his whole output.

73

It also demonstrates his most successful use of orchestral colour, without going beyond the limits of chamber music. With a tenor voice (oddly lying mostly lower than the baritone of *Sorrow's Lullaby*), string quartet, flute and cor anglais, it perfectly matches the mournful and sometimes poignant atmosphere, 'Let peewit call and curlew cry where they will.'

The common curlew, *Numenius arquata,* with its downward curving bill, known to the local people as either Gylfinhir (Long Bill)—Celtic philologists will recognise this as Gelvinak in Cornwall—or as Chwibanogl Fynydd (Mountain Whistler), would nest on the Welsh uplands on boggy moorland, where the grass and reeds are rough. It was noticed to have moved inland over Montgomeryshire by about 1907. The word curlew, coming from the Old French *courlieu,* is imitative of its plaintive call, sometimes a low whistle like a lament and sometimes a bubbling, rippling rising sound with identifiable notes. This was the call most commonly heard as the bird's general warning of the presence of a stranger.[9] Mr. Philip Owen, Q.C., when fishing in the mountain lakes above Llanbrynmair or down on the river Dyfi, would whistle to a curlew, he tells me, and it would call back. There is, amongst others, a Scottish tradition that this bird is a goblin, which uses its long beak like a pair of tongs for carrying off evil-doers at night.[10]

> 'I know of the leafy paths the witches take
> . . . out of the depths of the lake.'

Musicians have identified the interval of a rising sixth, lasting usually more than half a second—see diagram for a scientist's view.

The double-note call is usually thought of with a strong accent on the first syllable. It seems strange, therefore, that Philip, on the three occasions that he uses it, makes the second syllable accented and also longer than the first.

Cadman, W.A., 'Tales of a Wildfowler', illustr. Peter Scott.
Collins, 1957. 14 St James's Place, London. P.32.

By permission

Curlew call, p. 509.

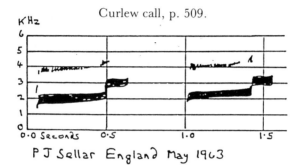

P J Sellar England May 1963

'Handbook of the Birds of Europe, etc.' Vol. 3: Waders to Gulls
I. Cramp, Stanley. O.U.P., 1983. *By permission*

The rising sixth is exaggerated to become a major seventh
in Philip's music and the other instruments overlap so as to
minimise its starkness.

Another call of repeated notes followed by a ripple on the
flute after letter B and at letter H, and again before the final
unaccompanied voice passage (with its solitary high A), is
thought by Dr. Copley[11] to represent the peewit, though this
may in fact have been inspired also by the curlew.

75

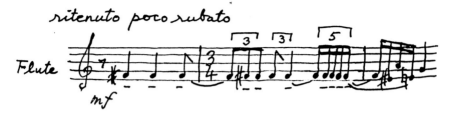

Again, Philip, like a painter, is using 'artist's licence', when we think of the frequent slow, sad dropping thirds. especially later.

This comes after the passage at letter X, which suggests the tuning of the lute. The song called *The Singer* is dated by Copley to 1919 and Tomlinson thinks it was written out in 1922.[12] It was not published until 1925, but it may be the first song which starts on the 'lute' chord. This chord, mostly of fourths, but with a third included, comes again many times in Philip's output[13] and is prominent at this stage in *The Curlew* in a developed form.

The *exact* notes of the lute strings occur at the ends of the first and second verses of *Cradle Song,* 1927 (bars 10 and 25).

The Curlew received a Carnegie Award in 1923, a most discerning decision at that time, and was published the following year.

With 'Covie's' financial help, there had been some not very successful concert promotion by Gerald Cooper, with whom Philip had travelled abroad in 1921. The dedication to Cooper, however, was transferred, after a quarrel, to Cecil Gray, in time for *The Curlew*'s appearance in print. My old copy of the score is inscribed to the new dedicatee, but the voice-and-piano copy has a paper slip pasted over the old one.

[1] Spelt in his day with 2 ms, this is a corruption of Pumlumon.

[2] Williams, Herbert, *Davies the Ocean. Railway King and Coal Tycoon* (University of Wales Press, Cardiff, 1991).

[3] Vaughan-Thomas, Wynford, *South & Mid Wales* (The New Shell Guides, ed. John Julius Norwich. Michael Joseph 1967).

[4] See Christiansen, Rex, *Forgotten Railways, North and Mid-Wales* (David & Charles 1976).

[5] Young, Percy, *Letters of Edward Elgar* (Geoffrey Bles 1956).

[6] Brit. Lib. ADD MS 57,962.

[7] Gray, *op.cit.,* pp. 159, 160.

[8] Symonds, J. and Grant, K., eds., *op.cit.,* p. 365.

[9] Forrest, H. E., *The Vertebrate Fauna of N. Wales* (Witherby, London 1907).

[10] Greenoak, F., *All the Birds of the Air* (Penguin 1981).

[11] Copley, *op.cit.,* p. 173.

[12] Peter Warlock Society Edn., Vol. 3 (Thames 1984).

[13] Parrott, Ian, 'Warlock & the Fourth' in *Music Review,* May 1966, pp. 130-2.

7. The Quarrelsome Warlock

Philip retained a considerable amount of understanding of Welsh music at its best. The fine 17th-century-sounding *Tros y Garreg* had been first published in Edward Jones's *Musical & Poetical Relicks of the Welsh Bards* in 1784 and later was called a 'Jig'. It makes a rather un-jig-like appearance as No. 4 in the *Folk-Song Preludes.* Philip's idea of Welsh music at its worst was mostly Victorian, which he considered vulgar, but he must have made an exception of the Irish-sounding hymn 'Ebenezer', written by Thomas Jones Williams in 1896 and known after 1905 as *Tôn-y-Botel,* because it was thought to have been washed up on the Welsh coast in a bottle. We have already noted that he used strange harmonies with it. Holbrooke had used it in his Celtic opera, *Bronwen,* and Vaughan Williams thought very highly of it.[1]

When Cecil Gray saw fit to quote Philip's letter to him of 19th November 1921, which includes the account of the performance that month of *Tôn-y-Botel* with Philip's own brand of harmony, he was compelled by the law of the land, of course, to alter or omit certain words. The request to play for the service had come not from 'the Rector' but, as can be seen in Philip's autograph, from 'the Rectum'. All the conventional rude words, such as 'bugger', are left out. However, it must have been his own personal decision to leave out, in line 6, 'though under no medical necessity' before 'I am being very abstemious here'; and, even more significantly, in line 11, Gray deliberately weakens the sense. The autograph, before suggesting an Irish booze-up, runs, 'Were the family to depart and you or some other genial soul to arrive in their place', but Gray avoids treading on corns, so the family is not mentioned. Gray also converts $C_2 H_5$ into $C_2 H_6 O$ (see Gray, p. 242, and compare with the autograph).[2] How many rare old books Philip found at Cefn-

Bryntalch is not known, but Gray[5] mentions *A plain and easy account of British Fungi* (1871) as the springboard for suggesting a week's debauch.

Philip's meticulous, small handwriting probably influenced Elizabeth Poston (1905-1987), a composer, especially of carols, who was associated with him for quite a time. The card (shown here p. 82) to Peter Boorman, then organist of St. David's, of 4th March 1958, demonstrates also the idea of using a note on the stave (E for Elizabeth) instead of a signature. Philip often did this sort of thing; Cecil Gray, for example, becoming 'Timpany' because of the orchestral direction 'Timpani in C and G'.

Dr. Copley quotes Miss Poston on Philip: 'It is perhaps both his strength and his weakness that Peter Warlock should so depend on his interpreters. With them lies the revelation of delight which he left us for legacy.'[4]

The relationship between Miss Poston and Philip seems to have been of a rather special nature and after his death a veil of silence gradually descended over its discussion. Nigel leaves us guessing on many things and some readers think that he may have been referring obliquely to this in his biography. Without much difficulty it may be supposed that Elizabeth Poston joined the ranks of those women who found Philip not only good-looking but attractive. What response she may have received is another matter.

Margaret Ashby[5] says that, in 1925 (when Miss Poston was a striking 20-year-old), she met the 'brilliant, but unstable, young composer born Philip Heseltine, who called himself Peter Warlock. Musically, Elizabeth was influenced by his work; on a personal level their friendship meant much to her.'

Whether she kept a copy of *The Curlew* open on her piano 'to the end of her life' is doubted by my friend, Peter Boorman, who frequently went to Rooks Nest, her home near Stevenage, but the music certainly made its mark and she arranged programmes later of Philip's compositions.

Rooks Nest had earlier been the home of the writer E. M. Forster, 1879-1970, who renewed his contact by his friendship with Elizabeth Poston. During the Second World War, Miss Poston, then at the B.B.C., had the secret service job of using gramophone records to broadcast coded messages to resistance movements in Europe.[6] After the War she went to North America researching American folksongs and in 1947 she was one of a panel which created the B.B.C.'s new Third Programme. When she died on 17th March 1987, her body, after a memorial service, was willed to medical science. Soon afterwards Rooks Nest was occupied by another composer, Malcolm Williamson, who seems to have rated her as a composer greater than either Philip or Vaughan Williams.[7] Miss Ashby tells me[8] that in her later years Elizabeth Poston was 'always fairly reticent about Peter Warlock, except for his influence on her music'.

In 1989 a compact disc, 'Sweet Echo' (Abacus ABA 604-2, sponsored by the Finzi Trust) was made of songs and carols by Elizabeth Poston and Peter Warlock. The Finzi Singers were directed by Paul Spicer. Miss Poston, described as a notable authority on Warlock, told Brian Rayner Cook, the baritone soloist, that she 'took pains to avoid the trap (as she put it) of being too influenced in her own composition by the English music of her youth'. A short article on her by Malcolm Rudland and David Cox appears in the *Peter Warlock Society Newsletter* No. 40 of February 1988.

After 1924, when he managed to fall off the rock of Montgomery Castle (NH p. 163), Philip was destined not to see his Welsh family home again, except for sporadic visits. On one of these in October 1928, feeling like a 'strayed ghost', he wrote, 'This solitary place is really beautiful . . . From here I seem to see the whole of the immediate past as through the wrong end of a telescope.'[9]

Earlier that year he had completed his superb setting of the anonymous 17th century *Eloré Lo,* which had also appeared in

Elizabeth Poston.

CEFN-BRYNTALCH,
ABERMULE,
MONTGOMERYSHIRE.

November 19ᵗ 1921

Most excellent of all possible kinds of birds!
I am indeed devastated to hear of your enforced abstention from the cordial comforts of those compounds derived from what I believe chemists and such like vulgar fellows call C_2H_5. It is a penance I myself could not by any means endure in London. The country, however, offers compensating delights to me and though under no medical necessity I am being very abstemious here, hardly attaining and never exceeding half a gallon of innocuous bitter ale per diem. This more than moderation is, all the same, due rather to solitude and the lack of anyone to share one's potations than to any other cause. Were the family to depart and you or some other genial soul to arrive in their place I should undoubtedly revive that good old Irish custom of sitting down to dinner in a locked room, throwing the key in the fire and continuing to drink until the fire had burned out and the metal cooled (to say nothing of one's own head) sufficiently to be handled and re-inserted in the key-hole. This is the kind of house that ought to contain rare old books and fine old wine.

From Philip's letter to Gray of 19 November 1921.

Thank you so much for writing, and, in advance, for return MS. (shortly to reach you in printed copy) which I hope may come in time when I go down & try the organ, with luck, over the weekend. After many delays, it's now being finished off & tuned. Till then send on your remaining bits, which make no great demands, but are quite fun, I think.

I'm so very glad you approve of the anthem setting: needless to say, I'm delighted that its first appearance is in your hands, & shd be thrilled if you did it in Welsh!

More anon - present thanks in lieu of equivalent of summon!

Elizabeth Poston to Peter Boorman of 4 March 1958.

Neuburg's anthology, *Lillygay*. It shows a fine understanding of poetic metre, being a complete vindication of the merits of 'regular' barring in music. Indeed, he instructs the singer to disregard bar-line accentuation. We can see him leaving the piano and stepping out of the drawing room at Cefn-Bryntalch,

Accents of words		>	>		>	>
		'In a garden so green			in a May morning'	
Accents for 6/8 or 3/4 time		>			>	

as he had done before, going through some of the croquet lawn and shrubbery (NH p. 97) to a secluded arbour to continue composing. What other composer, I wonder, would start with the word 'in' on the first note of a bar? 'Covie' would not allow the piano to be played in the afternoons and Philip was back in London by November. There are two final episodes in his life: Eynsford 1925-28; and London for his last two years.

Although the setting of an anonymous poem from *Wit and Drollery*, 1661, called 'The Jolly Shepherd', belongs to the Eynsford period, being composed in 1927, I am tempted to think of Philip's mind roving back to those wild scrambles over the bleak hills and crags of mid-Wales five years earlier. 'The life of a shepherd is void of all care-a, . . . he walketh all day in the cold-a' and, in the third verse, 'If cold doth oppress him to cabin goeth he-a.' Welsh shepherds working over large areas of mountain-side would need a cabin or tent (the Welsh word is 'lluest') for shelter, particularly under the severe stormy conditions with mists so often suddenly sweeping across. The remote lake Bugeilyn, not far from Dylife, means in fact 'Shepherd's Lake'.

In his letter to Gray of 14th June 1922, Philip mentions a somewhat severe uncle on the Covernton side living near Brilley (south of Knighton) and then suggests dossing down for the night at Dylife before trekking the 21 miles to the

Anchor, allowing two days for the journey because of the hills. He recommends the use of a compass and then 'strike up into the hills, across the Severn, past a farm called Cae-Lluest . . .' (This means 'Shepherd's Cabin Field') to Upper Camnant ('Crooked Brook'), near Kerry Hill, which used to belong to the Buckley Jones family.

Even more interesting in a way is the probability of a Welsh origin for the peculiar refrain:

'Trangdilla, trangdilla,
trang down a down dilla.'

and for the almost Italianate addition of an 'a' to all words at the ends of lines. Here is the equivalent part of the refrain to 'Bywyd y Bugail' (A Shepherd's Life) in *Y Flodeugerdd Gymraeg*.[10]

'Tra mynno, tra mynno
y cân pan ei tynno.'

where the feminine endings are a natural feature of Welsh and where there is precisely the same number of syllables. Yet more remarkable, by way of clinching the Welsh origin of *The Jolly Shepherd,* is the fact that the Welsh composer, E. T. Davies, published a setting of the poem a year *before* Philip's song. *Bywyd y Bugail* (The Happy Shepherd), with text said to be circa 1600, arranged by Ifor Williams and with an English version by Llew Tegid, was set by E. T. Davies (Director of Music at Bangor University College 1920-1943) and published by Hughes & Co., Cardiff, in 1926. If anything, it may be said that Llew Tegid's English translation is better than the version from *Wit and Drollery* with its nonsense refrain.

The drift of the poem, however, is clearly the same, with the scrip and flagon, dog and pipe,[11] etc. The equivalent to the third verse, which I have quoted, is: 'The foliage protects him from June's heat and swelter, The hedge or kind shanty in winter gives shelter'.

Evan Thomas Davies's sturdy modal theme bears no obvious resemblance to Philip's.

I have always resolutely resisted the temptation to fit any tunes in counterpoint to Elgar's 'Enigma' theme,[12] but now an opportunity arises to do something like it. Surely the Welsh harp-air, *Llwyn Onn* (The Ash Grove), with its tune based on chords (it is incorrect to describe it as a folk-*song*), could be supposed to be in Philip's mind as he identified himself with this phlegmatic sheep-minder. He uses a theme full of wide intervals, most unlike his usual conjunct or folk-like line. Melodies based on a broken chord formula, such as this, are uncommon in his output, says Dr. Copley.[13] So is it just a coincidence that some of it fits so well according to the unique Welsh technique of *'canu penillion'*, where a bard would improvise verses to a new tune over a harp-air?

As a boy Philip had stayed with an aunt, 'Covie's' sister Connie, who had married the rector, at Whitney-on-Wye[14] in Herefordshire. Lawrence Richings was rector there from 1902 to 1927. The old rectory is a pleasant many gabled Victorian house built for his predecessor, Henry Dew. This is just across the Welsh border, 15 miles south along Offa's Dyke from his mother's birthplace, Knighton, and about 5 miles from Clyro, home of the famous diarist, Kilvert (who is *not* quoted in *Merry-Go-Down*, see below). For old time's sake, Philip dedicated this song to an old friend, G. T. Leigh Spencer, who had then lived just across the Wye at Clifford.

Even if Welsh shepherds today still welcome a hut for shelter, English gamekeepers, whose methods have changed since Lawrence's *Lady Chatterley's Lover* (1928), no longer need them. Nor does the law of the land now ban the publication of such a novel as this one, which had to wait for more than 30 years to be treated as no longer obscene.

But for all his boyhood memories, Philip had persistently gone against his mother and his step-father's family in every way, sexual, occupational and social. Moreover, by his extremely odd will, he had cut himself off even from his own flesh and blood, his son, Nigel.

We should, perhaps, spare a moment to show some sympathy for the unwanted son, who grew up in the family home, his mother having disappeared immediately from the scene and his father almost oblivious to his presence—'This boy did not seem to belong to him' (NH p. 138)—until he too passed away during the boy's teens—'a "father" who meant nothing' (NH p. 162). 'Covie', the grandmother, became a mother to him and he gave 'Captain' (Montgomeryshire Volunteers) Walter the son he had wished for but never had (NH p. 91).

Although Nigel made a better job of getting on with 'Covie', Walter and their military associates than Philip had done, he *did* share with his father a genuine love of the Welsh countryside over which they both separately had roamed, the latter hunting rabbits with dogs (NH p. 18).

'Covie' bought off van Dieren with £6,000 to liberate her from the will (NH p. 166), but Nigel, inheriting an impoverished estate, wisely sold up and departed to 'foreign parts' (NH p. 97). Nigel remembered that the last farm to be sold, where he recalls going on picnics, was Cwm-y-Rhiwdre, near the original home of the Buckley Jones family at Mochdre. 'Covie' died in 1943 and Cefn-Bryntalch was sold by trustees in 1946 (NH p. 24), the next owners being Professor and

Mrs. Francis Halliday, sometime Head of the German Department at Swansea University College. They bought the house fully furnished, some surplus being sold at auction.

In the 50s, Barbirolli stayed with them when in May he came to conduct at the Montgomery County Music Festival, held in a converted aeroplane hanger in Newtown. The Hallidays left after thirteen years and, with a few more changes, the house passed to the present owners, the Nelsons.

From the style of writing of Nigel's biography it can be detected that some was written nearly forty years ago and, because of the law of libel, 'the manuscript lay in the office of my lawyer' (NH p. 5). The book, however, was finished in 1991. If this makes for a certain coy concealing of identities and some duplication here and there, it in no way detracts from its gripping impact.

The new book rings true, aiming not to debunk, but only to put a considerable record straight. If, for example, the son's picture of Delius and van Dieren, to name only two, sounds unduly hostile, one might compare it with Ernest Bradbury's milder summary: 'Delius's paternal musical influence was decisive. . . (then) van Dieren's music exercised an influence stronger than that of Delius.'[15]

Warlock-worshippers will have to get reconciled to the disclosure that their idol had feet of very sticky clay . . . though, of course, he sometimes wrote wonderfully strong music.

Foundation members of the Peter Warlock Society will admit that we enjoyed reading of Philip's squabbles and feuds, which led to the production of fifty scurrilous limericks,[16] but we never stopped then to think of what initial unease may have caused this dissipation of energy. 'He could write better . . . limericks, Priapian and other, than any man I have ever known,' wrote Robert Nichols, a poet with him at Oxford in 1913.[17] This energy was directed towards many unfruitful and indeed, with the enmities caused, positively harmful objects. It looks like the activity of an essentially weak and uncertain character.

In Malcolm Gillies's *Bartók in Britain*[18] we read that Frederick Corder, 1852-1932, an 'old school' member of staff at the Royal Academy of Music, wrote in 1914 'On the Cult of Wrong Notes',[19] in which Bartók's production was 'mere ordure'. I was able to point out to Mr. Gillies that one of Philip's limericks must have followed this.

> A young lady once told Frederick Corder
> How profoundly his music had bored her.
> She said, 'Percy Pitt
> Writes a good deal of shit
> But yours, Sir, is nothing but ordure.

Whatever reaction Philip might have expected from Corder, it was tactless, to say the least, to lampoon Percy Pitt, Director of Music at the B.B.C. at the crucial period, 1924 to 1929, who was interested in contemporary European music[10] and who appointed Edward Clark as programme planner in 1926. Pitt in 1886 had been a fellow music student in Leipzig with Delius, as noted by Philip in his biography.[21] He was succeeded as BBC Director of Music by Adrian Boult.

Unsure of himself, Philip frequently picked a quarrel with others and one suspects that he must have been jealous of his more successful contemporaries, particularly in the field of orchestral writing. He had already enjoyed 'taking the mickey' out of César Franck and even the giant Beethoven with his 'sacrilegious' parodies dating back to 1917 called *Cod-pieces*. Then, writing, for example, on Holst's *The Planets*, he refers to 'That Butchered Cosmos Again',[22] and, when Augustus John wrote to him on 29th July 1929, we read, 'We have Georges Auric here this weekend. A very good fellow— whatever you may say to his musical efforts.'[23] What did Philip say? Perhaps John had seen the limerick on 'Les Six', of which Auric was a member:

Piss is the sign of the Six
Though five of them only have pricks.
    The penis de Milhaud
    Pisses more than a kilo.
God damn their urethritic tricks.

This is an improvement on Aleister Crowley of 1904:

General paralysis
    Of the insane
Baffles analysis.
    Treatment is vain.
Never more rallies his
    System or brain.

The third line, 'baffles analysis', anticipates two of Philip's other limericks: one directed against Ursula Greville, who took over his magazine, *The Sackbut,* and the other, quoted in Gray,[24] on 'Young Girls who frequent picture palaces'. If Augustus John's Foreword to Gray's *Memoir*[25] is read again, we find not only that John was proposing to revive the rites of an ancient cult by a sacrifice in a church (a pleasantry?) but also that they failed to set out on a tour of Wales at the last fatal hour, so missed averting the final tragedy. In earlier letters of John we find the names of Crowley, Mudd and Hirsig appearing, since in 1924 Philip was asking for their addresses.

Norman Mudd, born Manchester 1889, at Trinity College, Cambridge in 1909, joined Neuburg's Pan Society, becoming a Crowley follower. Later, in South Africa, he came over to London in 1920 looking for Crowley at the Café Royal (but without success at the time).

It was said that when Crowley entered the Café Royal, a silence fell upon everyone, his cold, staring eyes set in his fat feminine face, with his shaved head, producing a response of awe. Philip, later, made a similar arresting impression with his 'derisive smile on his pale handsome features',[26] wrote Augustus John in Gray's *Memoir.*

In his own first autobiography, John says that when he first went to the Café Royal he used to observe a 'tall blond young man, usually accompanied by two or three females bearing portfolios and scrolls'. Philip's derisive, not reassuring, smile made him feel uncomfortable. 'He displayed remarkable conversational powers and a fund of curious knowledge . . . (but) it was impossible to remain unaware of the deeper side of this man's nature, try as he might to dissimulate it under a show of unproarious wit and effrontery.'[27]

Harriet Cohen, meeting him at the Glastonbury Festival in 1915, found two 'striking' young men. 'One, tall, handsome and bearded like an Elizabethan poet, was the gifted and fantastic-minded composer, Peter Warlock (Philip Heseltine); the other, his boon companion, the writer and critic Cecil Gray.'[28] Does she mean a year later, when Philip apparently first met Gray, or were they in Gloucestershire (see Gray's biography, pp. 100 and 125)? It looks as if Gray did not remember when he first met Philip, since Nigel (NH p. 113) puts it clearly in 1915.

Leah Hirsig was Crowley's current Scarlet Woman and to satisfy Crowley's peculiar perverse religion she had to be 'married' to Mudd. She was followed by Dorothy Olsen, a rich American devotee who was painted by Augustus John several times. By 1930 Leah Hirsig had passed out of Crowley's life and, in June 1934, Norman Mudd committed suicide in the sea off Guernsey.

The name of Tenby-born Sir Augustus John, R.A., 1878-1961, distinguished painter of portraits, including those of G. B. Shaw, Dylan Thomas and Delius (a drawing),[29] brings us back to our first theme of homage. Does a portrait painter, more than any other artist, fool the public by presenting his subject as a noble and upright character, just as impeccable to look at as to listen to? What would a portrait of his erstwhile friend Crowley look like?

After these somewhat sombre reflections arising out of some letters, usually short, from Augustus John to Philip, it is a pleasure to turn to one the other way about. Moreover it is to a letter which records Philip's unreservedly generous support of his more illustrious contemporary, Elgar, after reading Dent's cool appraisal in 1930 in Adler's *Handbuch der Musikgeschichte*. With enthusiasm Philip threw himself into drumming up support for Elgar in a characteristically vigorous way.

His letter[30] to Augustus John of 21st November 1930 runs, 'Would you care to sign the enclosed letter which is shortly to be circulated to the newspapers? It would be a great help if you would. G.B.S. [Shaw], Harty, Landon Ronald and many other friends of Elgar have signed, and we hope to get several more on the list.

'Are you in town now? It is months since I last saw you, and "The Antelope" [a Chelsea pub] is now quite impossible.'

Bernard Shaw actually added to the letter in question, 'Professor Dent should not have belittled his country by belittling the only great composer who is not dwarfed by the German giants.'[31]

Philip, when the letter appeared in *The Musical Times* of April 1931,[32] was dead. His energy, however, had been in evidence less than a month before the end (not the act, it would seem, of one contemplating suicide).

I remember personally feeling very indignant about the eccentric Dent only four years later, when for the 250th anniversary of the births of Bach and Handel, Sir Hugh Allen at Oxford celebrated both composers, but at Cambridge Dent celebrated—only Handel. Sir Hugh had been one of the Trustees of the Carnegie United Kingdom Trust, who passed *The Curlew* for publication in the 'Carnegie Collection of British Music' in 1924. Dent, on the other hand, had written his belittling article on Elgar, which appeared in the first edition of Adler that year, though it was not immediately noticed in Britain.

[1] Luff, Alan, *Welsh Hymns & their Tunes* (Stainer & Bell 1990).
[2] My chemistry friends tell me that Philip's original contained a misprint, but he meant to say that when water is added to ethylene it becomes ethyl alcohol.
[3] Gray, *op.cit.*, p. 287.
[4] Poston, Elizabeth, 'Peter Warlock, a perspective', *Newsletter—Journal of the Lancaster Music & Arts Club,* September 1945), p. 20.
[5] Ashby, Margaret, *Forster Country* (Flaunden Press 1991), p. 114.
[6] *Ibid.*, p. 131.
[7] *Ibid.*, p. 155.
[8] Letter to the author of 5th April 1993.
[9] Gray, *op.cit.*, p. 279.
[10] Cardiff, University of Wales Press 1931. See also *The Oxford Book of Welsh Verse,* 1962, p. 236.
[11] This means bagpipes. See 'Peter Warlock: A Centenary Celebration', ed. David Cox (Thames 1994).
[12] Redwood, Christopher, Ed., *An Elgar Companion* (Moorland 1982), pp. 82-90.
[13] Copley, *op.cit.*, p. 258.
[14] Tomlinson, Fred, Peter Warlock Society, Vol. 7, Preface.
[15] Bradbury, Ernest, 'Peter Warlock' in *The New Grove* (Macmillan 1980).
[16] See Mills, Patrick, 'A Warlock Obsession', *Peter Warlock Society Newsletter* 40, February 1988.
[17] Gray, *op.cit.*, p. 83.
[18] Gillies, *op.cit.*, pp. 20 & 21.
[19] Corder, Frederick, *Musical Quarterly,* July 1915.
[20] Kennedy, Michael, *Adrian Boult* (Hamish Hamilton 1987), p. 137.
[21] Warlock, Peter, *Frederick Delius* (Bodley 1923).
[22] Copley, *op.cit.*, p. 280.
[23] National Library of Wales, N.L.W. 18909 D.
[24] Gray, *op.cit.*, p. 277.
[25] Gray, *op.cit.*, pp. 11-15.
[26] Gray, *op.cit.*, p. 12.
[27] John, Augustus, *Chiaroscuro* (Cape 1952), p. 93.
[28] Cohen, Harriet, *A Bundle of Time* (Faber 1969), p. 31.
[29] Reproduced in the *Illustrated London News.* In December (last) issue of MILO (ed. Philip), December 1929.
[30] National Library of Wales, N.L.W. 22781 D Folio 110.
[31] Young, Percy, *Elgar O.M., op.cit.*, p. 235.
[32] Tomlinson, *op.cit.*, Vol. II.

8. The Drunkard Myth & Final Thoughts

Another activity, also, seemed to be filling Philip's mind during his final years: drinking. As part of his rejection of his family, he not only put on the facade of a riotous toper but took the view that the subject was worth writing about. Edward Clark told ApIvor that he was not, however, an 'alcoholic'.[1] This counterblast to the straitlaced attitude of his mother took shape as a book, 'Merry-Go-Down. A gallery of gorgeous drunkards through the ages. Collected for the use, interest, illumination and delectation of serious topers, by Rab Noolas and decorated by Hal Collins.'

Anyone drinking to excess in the neighbourhood of Abermule, such as 'Old Johns' of Garthmyl House and Dr. Phillips of Montgomery, was, of course, frowned on by his mother (NH p. 154). So what more natural than to compile this bawdy anthology under one of his many escapist pseudonyms, 'Rab Noolas' being Saloon Bar backwards? It was published in the same year as the Delius Festival, which Philip, with great dedication, helped to organise for Beecham (October 1929). 'Next to Beecham,' wrote Mrs. Jelka Delius to 'Covie', 'he really was the *soul* of the thing.' (NH p. 166).

Hal Collins (Te Akau), a Maori from New Zealand, became a sort of gentleman's gentleman to Philip and E. J. Moeran when they settled into a cottage in Eynsford early in 1925. According to Gray[2] they kept 'open house', including cats; and everyone who was in any way unusual or abnormal was sure of receiving a ready welcome. Whether this *ménage* gave Philip as much time for creative work as the more lavish life-style of Cefn-Bryntalch is doubtful, yet he continued with a huge output of literature, transcription and composition.

The composer, E. J. Moeran, partly Irish but born in London in the same year, out-lived Philip by twenty years. Ernest John Moeran was a pupil of Irish-born Sir Charles

MOTHERS' RUIN

There are certain old women of Maida Vale
Whom no prayers Bands of Hope ever pray'd avail
   To convert from the sin
   Of imbibing neat gin,
(Though they seem to be strangely afraid of ale).
                                [Rab Noolas.]

Cecil Gray.

94

E. J. Moeran.

Stanford and was conducted more than once by Irish-born Sir Hamilton Harty; and he clearly loved the Irish countryside as Philip did his Welsh. Although capable in his orchestral writing of sustaining much larger structures than Philip, the titles of such works as *In the Mountain Country* and *Lonely Waters* suggest an obvious affinity.

95

He had been a dispatch rider during the War and was wounded in the head, so his subsequent enthusiasm for motor-cycles may not have been quite as great as Philip's. He was also a song-writer, one of his best sets being the *Seven Poems of James Joyce* of 1929, written after his time with Philip at Eynsford. In 1945 he married Peers Coetmore, a cellist, and wrote a concerto for her.

Moeran and Philip produced a joint effort in 1926 with *Maltworms* to a sixteenth century text, 'I cannot eat but little meat', writing verse and chorus simultaneously in adjoining rooms.[3]

E. J. Moeran it was who appears to have told Nigel that van Dieren kept a huge collection (NH p. 31) of poisons in a cellar under his home. He died in County Kerry by drowning, apparently from a heart attack.

Collins was a specialist in woodcuts, producing a miniature of Philip and several illustrations for books and title pages of music. One particular claim to fame is that he provided a new set of words to Philip's well-known and popular folk-song arrangement, *Yarmouth Fair* (1921), when it was discovered that the original words were not traditional but copyright. He was also the dedicatee of the song, *Passing By*, composed in July 1928. He died of tuberculosis in 1929.

Merry-Go-Down was published by the Mandrake Press (and re-published by S. R. Publishers in association with Merrydown Wine in 1971). The mandrake is a plant once held to have magical powers and this is significant if we are to think of Philip still under the evil magic of Crowley. The Mandrake Press, a 'small and ephemeral firm',[4] founded by Edward Goldston and named by his Australian partner, P. R. Stephenson, had been set up not only to publish D. H. Lawrence[5] but also, eventually, Crowley. Two out of three parts of Crowley's *Confessions* appeared in 1930, but the firm soon went out of business. Neuburg reviewed Stephenson's apologia, *The Legend of Aleister Crowley,* in *The Freethinker.* Since Crowley insisted that the A of Aleister on the cover of

96

his *Confessions* should look like a phallus with testicles, the Mandrake salesman, not unexpectedly, had some difficulty in getting orders.

From 'The Great Beast' by John Symonds, p. 415.

Philip's intention also was to shock.

Some older Warlock enthusiasts may confess that they enjoyed first reading D. H. Lawrence, Aldous Huxley or James Joyce not for their literary quality but frankly because then they were 'outrageous' about sex, society or bad language. Some of the 'Olde Englyshe' in *Merry-Go-Down* seems rather tiresome today as does the concentration on what is 'not quite nice', but there are many unusual and interesting extracts, including George Borrow and James Joyce.

Having probably already read *Portrait of the Artist as a Young Man*,[6] the shocking *Ulysses* by Joyce, as first printed early in 1922, will have been in his mind when Philip wrote the Introduction to *The English Ayre*, since he starts with the wanderings of Leopold Bloom in the Dublin of 1904. During the following year hundreds of copies of *Ulysses* were either burnt by the New York Post Office or seized by the Folkestone Customs, so Philip was lucky to see it. Joyce's private language, moreover, matched his desire that Cornish should be *his* private language. Joyce's bad luck with the censors seems to have started as far back as 1905 with *Dubliners*. I had thought, incidentally, that the poem called 'Grog' on page 150 of Philip's book was by Dibdin, who wrote music to it, but it is labelled 'Early XIX cent. broadsheet'.

Philip had the boldness to wish to shock, as his contemporaries had done, yet felt compelled to hide behind the frosted glass of 'Rab Noolas'. The more joyous side of the book's contents is neatly displayed in the record, 'A Peter Warlock Merry-Go-Down', produced and directed by Fred Tomlinson in 1971.

The other novelist who aroused Philip's admiration was Aldous Huxley.

On 14th October 1930 the Porza Galleries in Berlin opened with an exhibition of paintings and drawings by Crowley of Leah Hirsig and Norman Mudd and, rather hastily, of Aldous Huxley, who, it will be remembered, had produced an amusing caricature of Philip in *Antic Hay* in 1923. 'I painted him like this to flatter him,' said Crowley, thinking Huxley had money. In this respect he was like van Dieren or Philip, but he was always selfishly ungrateful and, when people left him, he was more like Lawrence and revengeful. Crowley was declared bankrupt in 1935 and, after increasingly massive injections of heroin, died on 1st December 1947. If the smug Anglicanism of his mother and narrow rigidity of his father's sect produced such a Satanic life, can we be too surprised at the similar effect of Philip's parents? And it may be just as well that Cecil Gray never descended on Wales bringing a supply of hashish (NH p. 117). 'What my grandmother's reaction would have been,' wrote Nigel, 'to cannabis being smoked at Cefn-Bryntalch defies description.'

It is not entirely normal to quarrel with almost every person encountered and yet, in his short life, Philip managed to do just that. With his limited selection of enthusiasms and his many hatreds, Philip Heseltine, unlike Elgar with his vast friendships and small enmities, did not always realise where the true strength in his own music lay. He could reduce a

98

Delius score to a keyboard texture but was virtually incapable of producing a full orchestral score himself.

In 1917 his love of Scottish folk-song had actually produced a short chamber orchestra work, *An Old Song.* The tune is typically pentatonic, as is No. 5 (the last) of the *Folk-Song Preludes* (where it may be mentioned that a pentatonic melody on D is harmonised in B minor, not D major, as stated in the 'Introduction' to the modern edition). No. 5 is 'showy' in the middle, demonstrating Philip's casually easy technique and obvious disdain for what he was doing. No wonder he never wrote a concerto for anyone; he would have been too cynical about the fashionable 'lions of the keyboard' and their ilk— such as we still have—taking the limelight today. No. 5, as it happens, is based on an old Skye air, 'The Seagull of the Land-under-Waves' (from Mrs. Kennedy-Fraser, 1909).[7] Sir Granville Bantock, 1868-1946, used it in his *Hebridean Symphony,* which had its first performance in Glasgow in 1916. Did any of this get through to Philip, one wonders, while he was asleep at a concert? He could sleep through the noisiest compositions, but the *Hebridean Symphony,* said Gray,[8] was 'the only music that made him once stir uneasily in his seat'. *An Old Song,* however, is a dreamy introspective piece, looking at the mountainside much as Delius had looked at Norway in his early *Over the Hills and Far Away.* Other than songs or editing 'there was no sign of any broadening into other kinds of music . . . Would he have gone beyond the modest orchestral felicities of the *Capriol Suite?'* asks his son (NH p. 167).

Improving, however, on the shapelessness of Delius voice-parts, his music, says Gerald Cockshott, is 'less chromatic than some of van Dieren's melodies'.[9] Gerald Cockshott (1915-1979), an early member of the Peter Warlock Society and its chairman from 1963 to 1969, was quite discerning but like surprisingly many other commentators, either under-estimated or ignored the fruitful influence of Bartók. One of Cockshott's 'blind spots' was Elgar who, I seem to remember,

99

sounded to him like Boy Scouts singing in the middle of Birmingham. Was he perhaps thinking of the unmusical Yeats banning the setting of his poetry after hearing a solitary man's desire for even greater solitude sung by a thousand Boy Scouts?[10]

Turning to the Elizabethan period was, and still is, a form of escapism, but with all its psychological implications, this really did become for Philip an added source of strength in his own works. His style was in fact already unified in the early twenties and, if one wishes to dispel the notion of a dual personality, all that is needed is to compare the refrains of two songs. One, a setting in Wales of Neuburg's paranormally received words, being poignantly sad, the other, written when back in London, boisterously boozy:

'The Distracted Maid', 1922.

'Peter Warlock's Fancy', 1924.

Two carols of 1927, *What cheer? Good cheer!*, and *Where Riches is Everlastingly,* were dedicated the following year to his rich and pious stockbroker uncle, Evelyn Heseltine, 'in the hope that he might fork out a little dough at Christmas; but alas....'.[11]

On 3rd May 1930, 'Covie' and Walter attended Uncle Evelyn's funeral at the church he had built in memory of Arnold, Philip's father. In a letter to Delius of 29th September, Philip wrote that, of the £639,366 which had been left, 'not a penny came my way'. A month later, on behalf of her crippled husband, Jelka Delius replied, 'I was very sorry about your rich uncle [Evelyn] being so mean to you in his will. If you could only get a little something out of the final sale of Uncle Joe...'[12] She hoped Philip might eventually own one of his houses, but it was not be to. Three months after one funeral, 'Covie' and Walter joined the musicians, Bliss, van Dieren, Gray and Lambert and the poets, Bruce Blunt and Robert Nichols, at another. This, at Godalming Old Cemetery on 20th December, was of Philip himself.[13]

Looking back after all these years, is it surprising that his family had rejected him? He had, after all, abandoned the family name and taken on one which, for all the sardonic amusement it may have aroused in his own circle, must have been looked on with horrified suspicion by his mother, if not by Walter and the neighbours.

By the time Philip had returned to the scene of his ancestral home at the turn of the century, Wales had become a country of two languages: English for management, Welsh for labour; English in urbanised areas, Welsh in rural areas; English for the Anglican Church, Welsh for nonconformity. Always, as David Davies had observed (see Chapter 5), English was the language of power. It was against this background that Philip's obstinate study of Celtic languages showed for once that his opposition to the mid-Wales gentry had strength and decision.

So what do we have musically at the end of this centenary survey of a flawed genius?

Elgar is now established indisputably as the greatest of this British group. It was not always so. In my young days, Delius was thought of as more important, being promoted in particular by that brilliant conductor, Beecham, who, incidentally, was almost 'allergic' to Elgar. 'You must stop Sir Thomas conducting Elgar. He's fighting against it and will do himself an injury,' said his doctor to the secretary of the Royal Philharmonic Society. No doubt this attitude had been built up after, early on, Lady Elgar had formed a dislike of his conceited manner.

This study, sixty years afterwards, would not be complete without mentioning that in 1934, a few months before their deaths, Elgar and Delius met under conditions of the utmost cordiality[14] —a truly historic occasion.

In spite of the ministrations of some persistent and dedicated disciples, Delius has been slipping down the rungs of the ladder which ascends to universal acclaim, while Peter Warlock's many exquisite songs have kept his name fresh in the hall of fame at the top of the ladder, albeit in a small alcove away from a world view. It might well be said that Philip has left a 'living name behind', while some of his much-vaunted contemporaries 'weave but nets to catch the wi - n d.' These words of John Webster, 1580-1630, come at the end of Philip's fine but difficult setting, *All the Flowers of the Spring,* a dirge for the shrouding of the Duchess of Malfi, published by Boosey in 1924, and take us back to those bleak Welsh mountainsides. It is almost *avant-garde* in its treatment of 'wind', the prolongation of the first syllable and the 16 bars moaning, vocalising on the consonant 'n' before the final 'd' at the end of the page.

So, like Augustus John, after a 'repressive' Welsh religious upbringing, Philip became a persistent if guilty protester.

Did the Anglicised Welsh upper-classes turn him to the Celtic languages?

Did family shooting-parties turn him to pacifism?

Did respectable religion turn him to atheism?

Did conventional education turn him towards becoming a 'magus'?

Did their legal unprintability turn him to censored 'four-letter' words?

Did social taboos turn him to 'free love'?

Did prohibition turn him to drink? (Davies, 'top sawyer', had actually turned the entire village of Llandinam teetotal.)

Did insipid literature turn him to 'shocking' novelists?

Did 'showy' music turn him to 'modernist' composers?

Did the 'down-to-earth' turn him to the extra-sensory?

Did the obedience to his mother of dogs and ponies turn him to cats?

Did being out of tune with the times turn him to the 16th century? Could there be anything more for him to turn against?[15]

It will have been observed that I am not a Warlock-worshipper. May it not be, in conclusion, that the modest Gustav Holst, with his Indian-inspired *Savitri* of 1908[16] and Apocrypha-inspired *Hymn of Jesus* of 1919—with no skeletons in the cupboard—is the most new-sounding of this bunch of composers celebrated in 1994? Elgar for High Noon, Delius for Sunset, Warlock for Night—he set Belloc's *The Night* in 1927—and Holst for unassuming newness in the Dawn?[17]

Delius (in about 1897).

103

Sir Edward Elgar, Bart., O.M.   Gustav Holst.

There's something for the uncritical worshipper to mull over.

> 'Fold your great wings about my face,
> Hide dawning from my resting place,
> And cheat me with your false delight,
> Most Holy Night.'
>
> Hilaire Belloc, 1870-1953

Here is a poem by Nigel, which appeared in *Modern Welsh Poetry*[18] in 1944:

BARTER OUR NORTHERN DARKNESS

Can you picture the decision
that will free us beyond the day?
the size of the night is an orbit
beating below the households.

O singer who treads the bare
rocks of the south, barter
our northern darkness for your
stinging song that breaks the houses.

There is something for the sympathetic reader to contemplate.
Not a split personality, who left 'the tavern of life at his own
leisure', as Cecil Gray would have had us believe, Philip was
indeed sometimes 'mixed-up'. Although not of Celtic blood,
despite his mother being born on the Welsh side of the
border, he did show some of the volatile make-up of the
Welsh. Perhaps, as recorded in 'Joan's Ale' in 1780 (*Merry-Go-Down*, p. 87), he was like the 'Welch-man' who entered
the tavern 'with Joy and Sorrow mixt'.

As I finish writing about Philip Heseltine and his turbulent
life, the curlews are to be heard still accentuating with their
mournful cry the loneliness of the bare Welsh mountain-tops
in the wintry wind. These gave a solitary composer, with his
'bough-withering' dreams, some solace as he sought to
escape from his family and the many other disruptive
influences.

[1] ApIvor, Denis, Letter to *Peter Warlock Society Newsletter* 39, July 1987, p. 4.

[2] Gray, *op.cit.*, p. 255.

[3] Cockshott, Gerald, 'E. J. Moeran's Recollections of Peter Warlock' (*Musical Times*, March 1955).

[4] Symonds, John, *op.cit.*, p. 413.

[5] Moore, Harry T. and Roberts, Warren, *D. H. Lawrence and his World*, 1966.

[6] Gray, *op.cit.*, p. 276.

[7] See Introduction by Fred Tomlinson to *Peter Warlock. Folk-Song Preludes* (Thames edition, no date).

[8] Gray, *op.cit.*, p. 259.

[9] Cockshott, Gerald, in *Music & Letters*, July 1940.

[10] Gray, *op.cit.*, p. 248.

[11] Tomlinson, Fred, *op.cit.*, Vol. I, p. 44.

[12] Quote from this letter by courtesy of Raymond Monk.

[13] Tomlinson, Fred, *op.cit.*, Vol. I, p. 44.

[14] Redwood, Christopher, ed., *A Delius Companion* (J. Calder 1967, rev. 1980).

[15] See also ApIvor, Denis, 'P.H.: a Psychological Study, *op.cit.*

[16] Parrott, Ian, 'Holst's *Savitri* and Bitonality' in *Music Review,* November 1967.

[17] Philip himself thought of Beethoven as morning, Wagner as high noon and Delius as the sunset of Romanticism (*Delius,* p. 130).

[18] Rhys, Keidrych, ed., *Modern Welsh Poetry* (Faber 1944).

Bibliography

Allsobrook, David, *Music for Wales,* University of Wales Press, 1992.
Aplvor, Denis, 'Philip Heseltine (Peter Warlock): A Psychological Study', *Music Review,* May 1985; 'Bernard van Dieren', *Music Review,* November 1986; Letter to *Peter Warlock Society Newsletter,* July 1987.
Cox, David, (ed.) *Peter Warlock: A Centenary Celebration,* Thames 1994.
Copley, I. A., *The Music of Peter Warlock. A Critical Survey,* Dobson 1979; *A Turbulent Friendship* (D. H. Lawrence & Philip Heseltine), Thames 1983.
Fitzgibbon, Constantine, *The Life of Dylan Thomas,* Dent 1965.
Foreman, Lewis, ed. *From Parry to Britten,* Batsford 1987.
Fuller, Jean Overton, *The Magical Dilemma of Victor Neuburg,* W. H. Allen 1965. rev. Mandrake (Oxford) 1990.
Gillies, Malcolm, *Bartók in Britain,* O.U.P. 1989.
Gray, Cecil, *Peter Warlock: A Memoir of Philip Heseltine* (with contributions by Sir Richard Terry, Robert Nichols and Augustus John), Cape 1934.
Heseltine, Nigel, *Capriol for Mother: A Memoir of Philip Heseltine (Peter Warlock) and his family by his son,* Thames 1992. See also *Peter Warlock Society Newsletter 46* of March 1991.
Tales of the Squirearchy Druid Press 1947.
Tales of the Landless Gentry. A sequel (some in Penguin, *New Writing,* Faber, etc).
Heseltine, Philip (with Cecil Gray), *Carlo Gesualdo, Musician and Murderer,* Kegan Paul 1926.
Heseltine, Philip (Peter Warlock), *The English Ayre,* O.U.P. 1926; *Frederick Delius,* Bodley 1923, rev. 1952.
'Modern Hungarian Composers' *Musical Times,* March 1922.
Huxley, Juliette, *Leaves of the Tulip Tree,* John Murray 1986.
John, Augustus, *Chiaroscuro,* Cape 1952 (also *Finishing Touches* 1964).
Jones, Daniel (ed.) *Dylan Thomas: The Poems,* Dent 1971.
Lambert, Constant, *Music Ho! A Study of Music in Decline,* Faber 1934.
Luff, Alan, *Welsh Hymns and Their Tunes,* Stainer & Bell 1990.
Moore, Harry T. & Roberts, Warren, *D. H. Lawrence and His World,* 1966.

Motion, Andrew, *The Lamberts. George, Constant & Kit,* Chatto & Windus 1986.

Parrott, Ian, *The Spiritual Pilgrims,* Christopher Davies 1968; 'Holst's *Savitri* & Bitonality', *Music Review,* November 1967.

Redwood, Christopher, *A Delius Companion,* J. Calder 1976, revised 1980; *An Elgar Companion,* Moorland 1982.

Shead, Richard, *Constant Lambert,* 1973, revised Thames 1987.

Smith, Barry, *Peter Warlock: The Life of Philip Heseltine (1894-1930),* O.U.P. 1994.

Symonds, J. & Grant, K. (eds.), *The Confessions of Aleister Crowley. An Autohagiography,* Hill & Wang (72 Fifth Ave, New York) 1970. Bantam 1971.

Symonds, John, *The Great Beast. A Life & Magick of Aleister Crowley,* Rider 1951, Macdonald 1971, Mayflower (Frogmore, St Albans, Herts.) 1973.

Tomlinson, Fred, *A Peter Warlock Handbook,* Triad Press, Vol. I 1974, Vol. II 1977; *Warlock & Delius,* Thames 1976; *Warlock & Van Dieren,* Thames 1978; *Warlock & Blunt,* Thames 1981.

Williams, Herbert, *Davies the Ocean. Railway King & Coal Tycoon,* University of Wales Press 1991.

Young, Percy M. *Elgar O.M. A Study of a Musician,* Collins 1955; *Letters of Edward Elgar,* Geoffrey Bles 1956; *A History of British Music,* Benn 1967.

Index

ill = illustration
n = note

Abermule, 9, 11, 20, 29-31, 41, 61, 67, 68, 93
Aberystwyth, 29, 30, 55
Abra-Melin, 28
Adler's 'Handbuch', 91
Akau, Te see Collins, Hal
Alldrith, Keith, 12
Allen, Sir Hugh P., 91
Allen, William R., 37, 55ill
'Anchor Inn' (Shropshire border), 65, 70, 84
'Antelope, The' (Chelsea), 91
ApIvor, Denis, 13, 35, 40, 93
    'Philip Heseltine: a Psychological Study', 14n, 105n
Aran Fawddwy, 66
Arbeau, Thoinot
    'Orchésographie', 60
Ashby, Margaret, 79, 80
Ashton, Frederick, 10
Augustine of Hippo, Saint, 47
Auric, Georges, 88

Bach, J. S., 20, 91
Baillot, Juliette see Huxley, Juliette
Baker, Frank, 14n
Banner, Betty see Crawshaw, Betty
Bantock, Sir Granville
    Hebridean Symphony, 99
Barbirolli, Sir John, 87
Barnby, Sir J., 44
Bartók, Béla, 24, 28-31, 30ill, 72, 99
    Allegro Barbaro, 29
    Bear Dance, 29, 31
    Miraculous Mandarin, The, 31
    Violin Sonata No 2, 29
Beaumont, Cyril, 60
Beckhard, Robert, 64n
Beddoes, Thomas Lovell, 38
Beecham, Sir Thomas, 93, 101

Beechings, Dr, 67
Beethoven, L. van, 11, 88
    'Archduke' Trio, 29
Belloc, Hilaire, 56, 103, 104
Berlin, 98
Birmingham, 18, 100
Blackwood, Algernon, 50
Blavatsky, Helena Petrovna, 47
Bliss, Sir Arthur, 35, 101
Blunt, Bruce, 37, 58, 101
Bodley, S. J., 15, 18
Boleskine, 49
Boorman, Peter, 79, 82ill
Boosey & Co., 102
Borrow, George, 97
    'Wild Wales', 66, 67
Boult, Sir Adrian, 35, 56, 88, 92n
Bradbury, Ernest, 87
Brilley (Herefordshire), 83
Brittany, 60
Broadstairs, 11, 68
Bryant, Nigel, 64n
Bryn Celli Ddu (Anglesey), 73ill
Buckley-Williames, Catherine see Jones, Catherine
Budapest, 29, 31
Bugeilyn Lake, 67, 72, 72ill, 83
Burley, Rosa, 26
Burma, 19
Busoni, F., 39

Cadman, W. A., 75ill
Caersws, 68
Camberley, 9, 25
Cambridge, 47, 91
    Trinity College, 49, 89
Cammell, C. R., 51
Carnegie Collection of British Music, 91
Cefn-Bryntalch, 9, 11, 15ill, 18, 24, 29, 31, 41, 43, 63, 68, 69, 78, 79, 82ill, 83, 86, 93, 98
Ceiriog see Hughes, John
'Celtia', 59

'Celtica', 64n
Celtic culture, 28, 49, 54, 57-59, 69, 70, 97, 101
Chamberlain, Arthur, 18
Chamberlain, Joseph M.P., 18
Chelsea *see* London
Christiansen, Rex, 77n
Christie, Agatha, 36
Clark, Edward, 88, 93
Clements, Charles, 29, 55ill
Clifford (Herefordshire), 86
Clyro (Powys), 85
Clywedog reservoir, 67
Cockshott, Gerald, 42n, 99, 105n
Coedarhydyglyn, 69
Coetmore, Peers, 96
Cohen, Harriet, 90, 92n
Collins, Brian, 52n
Collins, Hal (Te Akau), 93, 94ill, 96
Cologne, 31
Cook, Brian Rayner, 80
Cooke, Evelyn, 55ill
Cooper, Gerald, 77
Cooper, Tom, 31
Copley, Dr Ian, 13, 27, 59, 79
    'The Music of Peter Warlock', 14n, 59, 64n, 75, 76, 85
    'A Turbulent Friendship', 27, 64n
Corder, Frederick. 88
Courtney, Tom, 38
Covernton, Dr Charles (grandfather), 11
Covernton, Connie *see* Richings, Connie
Covernton, Edith *see* Jones, Edith Buckley
Covernton, uncle, 83
'Covie' *see* Jones, Edith Buckley
Cox, David, 10, 80, 92n
Cramp, Stanley, 75ill
Crawshaw, Betty (née Banner), 60, 61
Crewe, Thomas de, 64
Crewe-Read, Capt O. M., 63
Crewe-Read, Col R. O., 60, 63
Crichton, Ann, 61
Crowley, Aleister, 28, 37, 44, 47, 48ill, 49-51, 72, 73, 89, 90, 96, 97ill, 98
    'Confessions', 47, 96, 97

'Daily Mail', 14
D'Aranyi, Jelly, 29, 30ill, 33n

David, Jacques Louis, 11
Davies, David, first Lord, 67
Davies, David, third Lord, 64
Davies, David, 'top sawyer', 54, 64, 67, 101, 102
Davies, Eiluned, 39
Davies, Lady Eldrydd (née Dugdale), 54
Davies, Evan Thomas, 84
    Bywyd y Bugail, 84
Davies, Gwendoline, 18, 54
Davies, Hubert, 29
Davies, Margaret. 18, 54
Davies, Michael, second Lord, 54
Davies, Sir (H.) Walford, 29, 31, 54-56
De La Noy, Michael, 12
Delius Festival, 93
Delius, Frederick, 9, 13, 20, 24, 28, 32, 52, 56, 70, 73, 87, 88, 90, 93, 99, 100-102, 103ill
    Arabesk, An, 50
    Over the Hills & Far Away, 99
    Requiem, 58
Delius, Jelka, 93, 101
Dent, Prof Edward J., 91
Dew, Rev Henry, 85
Dibdin, Charles, 98
Dieren, Bernard van, 12, 24, 28, 32, 35-41, 44, 36ill, 86, 98, 99, 101
    Piccolo Pralinudettino Fridato, 39
    String Quartet No 5, 39
    Tailor, The, 23
Dieren, Bernard J. van (Junior), 35, 36ill
Dieren, Frida van (née Kindler), 35, 39
Dolfor (Powys), 20
Dolgellau (Gwynedd), 37
Donne, John, 49
Dowbiggin, Arnold, 40
Dublin, 25, 31, 72, 97
Dugdale, Barbara *see* Lewis, Barbara
Dugdale, Eldrydd *see* Davies, Lady Eldrydd
Dugdale, Riba, 62
Dyfi, river, 74
Dylife (Powys), 65, 66ill, 67, 71ill, 83

Elgar Birthplace Trust, 35
Elgar, Lady (Caroline) Alice, 43, 102

Elgar, Sir Edward, 9, 10, 18, 24, 43, 54, 55, 57, 91, 98, 99, 101-103, 104ill
  Apostles, The, 55, 58
  Cello Concerto, 55
  Enigma Variations, 26
  Grania and Diarmid, 50
  Violin Concerto, 26
Elgar Society, 12, 41n
El Greco, 40
Eton College, 20, 23, 29
Eynsford, 83, 93, 96

Fachiri, Adila (née d'Arányi), 30ill, 33n
Fellowes, Dr Edmund H., 52
Fenby, Eric, 70
Fletcher, John, 56
'Flodeugerdd Gymraeg, Y', 84
Florida, 56
Folkestone, 97
Foreman, Lewis, 39
Forrest, H. E., 77n
Forster, E. M., 80
Franck, César, 88
'Freethinker, The', 96
Fuller, Jean Overton, 50, 53n

Garsington Manor, 25, 26ill, 28, 33n
Garthmyl (Powys), 61, 93
Gesualdo, Carlo, Prince of Venosa, 36, 38
Gillies, Malcolm, 88
  'Bartók in Britain', 23n, 88
Glasgow, 99
Glastonbury Festival, 90
Godalming, 101
Golden, Ruth, 51
Goldston, Edward, 96
Grainger, Percy, 70
Grant, Kenneth, 53n, 77n
Gray, Cecil, 13, 24, 27, 30, 32, 36-38, 40, 41, 51, 60, 65, 66, 68, 70, 77, 79, 83, 90, 101, 105
  'Musical Chairs', 33n
  'Peter Warlock. A Memoir', 13, 15, 20, 28, 33n, 42n, 58, 77n, 78, 79, 89, 92n, 93, 99, 105n
Greenoak, F., 77n
Gregynog Chair of Music, 35

Gregynog Choir, 55ill
Gregynog Hall, 18, 33n, 37, 54, 55, 55ill, 69
Greville, Ursula, 89
Grez-sur-Loing, 13
Griffith, A. Troyte, 70
Grove's Dictionary, 92n
Guernsey, 90
Gurney, Ivor, 56
'Gwas Myhal' see Jenner, Henry

Halliday, Prof Francis, 87
Handel, G. F., 91
Harlech, 55
Harman, Dr B. N., 18
Harrow School, 24
Harty, Sir Hamilton, 91, 95
Harwood, Ronald
  'Poison Pen', 38
Haydn, Joseph, 56
Heber, Bishop R., 68
Heine, Heinrich, 37
Hereford, 70
Heseltine, Arnold (father), 10, 11, 15, 100
Heseltine, Arthur ('Joe') (uncle), 13, 101
Heseltine, Edith (mother) see Jones, Edith Buckley
Heseltine, Evelyn (uncle), 10, 100, 101
Heseltine, Florence, 10
Heseltine, Irene, 51
Heseltine, Lucy ('Bobby'), née Channing ('Puma') (wife), 24, 61
Heseltine, Nigel (son), 9, 25, 26, 41, 60, 62-64, 86
  'Barter our Northern Darkness', 104
  'Capriol for Mother', 9, 14n, 32, 35, 41, 52, 54, 56, 64, 87
  'Dafydd ap Gwilym', ed., 54
  'Tales of the Squirearchy', 54
Heseltine, Peter (son), 24, 25
Heseltine, Philip ('Peter Warlock')
  birth, 9, 10, 105
  childhood, 10, 11, 15, 19, 20, 21ill
  family move to Wales, 11
  Eton, 20, 23, 24, 29
  Christ Church, 20, 87

marriage, 24
called himself 'Peter Warlock', 28,
44, 46ill, 79, 101
in Cornwall, 28, 57-59
in Ireland, 28, 31, 56, 72
pacifist, 20, 56, 57, 102
'Welsh' period, 1921-24, 44, 65-77,
78, 80, 102
Eynsford period, 83, 93, 96
death, 34-41, 55, 86, 89, 91, 101
edits 'The Sackbut', 29, 89
limerick writer, 87-89, 94ill
influence of Celtic languages and
folk-lore, 28, 49, 51, 52, 57-60,
66-69, 78, 83-85, 97, 99
influence of Christianity, 23, 57, 58,
101, 102
influence of curlew, 70, 74-77, 105
influence of drinking, 13, 20, 23, 41,
93, 94ill, 96, 98
influence of magic, 28, 32, 44, 47,
49, 50, 72, 73ill, 89, 97, 102
influence of sixteenth and seventeenth
centuries, 49, 52, 58, 76, 80, 83, 84,
100, 102, 103
Compositions
Adam Lay Ybounden, 63
After Two Years, 55ill
All the Flowers of the Spring, 102
Along the Stream, 44
Balulalow, 58
Bethlehem Down, 58
Candlelight, 39
Can Nadelek (Cornish Christmas Carol),
59
Capriol, 9, 10, 33n, 60, 99
Captain Stratton's Fancy, 23
Carillon Carilla, 58
Chanson du Jour de Noël, 58
Cod-pieces, 88
Corpus Christi, 57
Cradle Song, 43, 76
Cricketers of Hambledon, The, 23
Curlew, The, 28, 50, 72-77, 75ill,
79, 91
Distracted Maid, The, see Lillygay
Eloré Lo, 80, 83
First Mercy, The, 45, 58

Folk-Song Preludes (5 pieces), 31, 51,
78, 99
Fox, The, 37, 55ill
Frostbound Wood, The, 37
Good Ale, 23
In an Arbour Green (1922), 44
Jolly Shepherd, The, 83-86, 85ill
Liadain & Curither, 72
Lillygay (5 songs), 43, 50, 100 ill
Maltworms (with E. J. Moeran), 96
Milkmaids, 49
My Gostly Fader, 47
My Own Country, 56
Night, The, 103
Old Song, An, 99
Passing By, 96
Peter Warlock's Fancy, 100ill
Piggesnie, 55ill
Singer, The, 76
Sleep, 56
Sorrow's Lullaby, 38, 74
Spring of the Year, 55ill
Tyrley Tyrlow, 58
What Cheer? Good Cheer! 100
Where Riches is Everlastingly, 100
Yarmouth Fair, 96
Writings
'Carlo Gesualdo', 36
'English Ayre, The', 76ill, 97
'Frederick Delius', 32, 33n, 58,
64n
'Merry-Go-Down' (by 'Rab Noolas'),
85, 93, 94ill, 96-98, 105
Himalayas, 47
Kangchenjunga, 73
Hirsig, Leah, 89, 90, 98
Holbrooke, Joseph
Bronwen, 78
Hold, Trevor, 49
Holst, Gustav, 9, 54, 103, 104ill
Hymn of Jesus, 103
Planets, The, 88
Savitri, 103
Hooson, Lady Shirley, 32
Hotel Brighton, see Paris
Hughes & Co., Cardiff, 84
Hughes, John ('Ceiriog'), 68
Humphreys, Charles, 61, 64n

Humphreys, Charles Martin Strick, 60, 61
Humphreys, Christmas, Q.C., 61
Humphreys, Stella, 61
Huxley, Aldous, 23, 28, 97
  'Antic Hay', 23, 98
Huxley, Julian, 25
Huxley, Juliette (née Baillot), 25, 86

'Illustrated London News', 92n
India, 19
Inglis, Brian, 63

Jacobsen, J. P., 50
Jenner, Henry ('Gwas Myhal'), 59
John, Sir Augustus, 28, 88-91, 92n, 102
Johns, 'Old', Garthmyl House, 93
Johnson, Pamela Hansford, 51
Jones, Catherine (née Buckley-Williames), 17ill, 19, 20
Jones, Dr Daniel, 51, 60
  ed., 'Dylan Thomas: The Poems', 53n
  Sonata for Kettledrums, 51
Jones, Edith Buckley ('Covie', née Covernton, Mrs Arnold Heseltine) (mother), 10, 11, 15, 19, 20, 22ill, 24-27, 31, 32, 37, 43, 52, 57, 61, 63, 68, 70, 72, 78, 83, 85, 86, 93, 98, 100, 101, 102, 105
Jones, Edward
  'Musical & Poetical Relicks', 78
Jones, Brig-Gen Lumley, 18, 19, 20, 68
Jones, Parry, 37
Jones, Richard Edward, 15, 17ill, 18
Jones, Robert
  What if I seek, arr. Warlock, 55ill
Jones, Dr Thomas, C.H., 35
Jones, Walter Buckley (step-father), 11, 15, 18-20, 22ill, 26, 31, 37, 55, 57, 68, 72, 86, 98, 100, 101
Jones, Col Whitmore, 18, 19
Joyce, James, 96, 97
  'Dubliners', 98
  'Portrait of the Artist as a Young Man', 97
  'Ulysses', 97

Kennedy, Michael, 25, 26, 92n
Kennedy-Fraser, Marjorie
  Hebridean Songs, 51, 99
Kerry (Powys), 62
Kerry Hill, 84
Kilvert, Rev F., 85
Kindler, Frida see Dieren, Frida van
Kington, Beryl, 64n
Knighton (Powys), 11, 66, 70, 85

Ladmirault, Paul, 60
Lambert, Constant, 37, 101
  Horoscope, 38
  'Music Ho!', 38
  Piano Concerto, 39
Lampeter, 70
Lawrence, D. H., 24, 27, 28, 51, 57, 59, 96, 97
  'Lady Chatterley's Lover', 86
  'Rainbow, The', 27
Leamington, 47
Leipzig, 88
Lévi, Eliphas, 28
Lewis, Barbara, 55
Lewis, Mrs Hugh, 64n
Lewis, Peter, 55, 64n
Llanbrynmair, 67, 74
Llandinam, 54, 64, 67
Llandyssil (Powys), 9, 19, 31, 61
Llanfyllin, 54
Llanidloes, 32, 55
Lloyd George, David, 35
Llwyn Onn (The Ash Grove), 85, 85ill
'Locomotive, The', 68
London, 9, 18, 72, 83, 100
  B.B.C., 38, 80, 88
  British Museum, 59
  Café Royal, 44, 89, 90
  Chelsea, 10, 11, 19, 34, 34ill, 91
  Great Exhibition of 1851, 18
  Hammersmith, 49
  Royal Academy of Music, 88
  Royal Philharmonic Society, 101
  Savoy Hotel, 10
  University, 23
Ludlow, 66, 68
Luff, Alan, 92n
Lygon, Lady Mary, 26

Machynlleth, 66
Manchester, 38, 89
Mandrake Press, 96
Masefield, John, 23
Maugham, W. Somerset
  'The Magician', 47
Mexico, 47
Meyers, Jeffrey, 27, 33n
Milhaud, Darius, 89
Mills, Patrick, 34, 59, 60, 64n
'Milo', 92n
Mitchell, John, 36
Mochdre (Powys), 15, 86
'Modern Welsh Poetry', 104
Moeran, E. J., 35, 40, 93, 95ill
  Cello Concerto, 96
  In the Mountain Country, 95
  Lonely Waters, 95
  Seven Poems of James Joyce, 96
Monk, Raymond, 36ill, 53n, 105n
Montgomery (Powys), 9, 61, 67, 80, 93
Montgomeryshire County Music
  Festival, 87
Moore, Gerald, 64n
Moore, Harry T., 38, 42n
Morrell, Julian, 25, 26ill
Morrell, Lady Ottoline, 25, 28, 33n,
  57
Morrell, Philip, 25
Motion, Andrew, 33n, 38
Mudd, Norman, 89, 90, 98
'Music & Letters', 105n
'Musical Quarterley', 92n
'Music Review', 14n, 106n
'Musical Standard', 13
'Musical Times', 42n, 105n

Nant-y-moch reservoir, 67, 70
National Library of Wales, 92n
Nelson, E., 87
Nettlefield, John, 18
Neuburg, Kathleen Rose (née Goddard),
  49
Neuburg, Victor, 43, 45ill, 49-52, 89,
  96, 100
  'Larkspur', 49
  'Lillygay', 50, 83
'New Age, The', 52n

Newport (Gwent), 50
Newtown, 15, 18, 20. 31, 87
New York, 97
New Zealand, 93
Nichols, Robert, 57, 87, 101
Noel, Malcolm, 42n
Noy, Michael de la *see* De la Noy

Olsen, Dorothy, 90
Onslow, Arthur Loftus, 32
Onslow, Mabel, 32
Orr, Joan (née Crewe-Read), 63, 64
Oswestry, 68
Owen, Philip, Q.C., 74
Owens, Richard, 18
Oxford, 23, 47
  Christ Church, 23. 24
  'Oxford Book of Welsh Verse', 92n

Paris, 10, 60
  Hotel Brighton, 10
Parrott, Prof Ian, 14n, 24, 33n, 41n,
  64n
  'Holst's Savitri & Bitonality', 106n
  'Spiritual Pilgrims, The', 64n
  'Warlock & the Fourth', 77n
Parry, Sir C. Hubert H., 58
Peache, Barbara, 41
Peter Warlock Society, 9, 12, 34, 87, 99
Peter Warlock Society Journal, 10
Peter Warlock Society Newsletter, 40,
  42n, 52n, 80, 92n, 105n
Peter Warlock Society Edition, 77n,
  105n
Phillips, Dr, 93
Pitt, Percy, 88
Plynlimon (Pumlumon), 65, 66ill, 70
Poston, Elizabeth, 79, 80, 81ill, 82ill
Powell, Anthony, 32
Powick
  Pauper Lunatic Asylum, 10
Prague, 31
'Puma' *see* Heseltine, Lucy

Quilter, Roger
  Trollie Lollie, 49

Rab Noolas *see* Heseltine, Philip
Read, John, 64

Redwood, Christopher, 92n
Rhys, Keidrych, 106n
Richings, Connie, née Covernton (aunt), 85
Richings, Rev Lawrence, 85
Roberts, Warren, 105n
Rogers, Winthrop, 53n, 59
Ronald, Sir Landon, 91
Rosicrucians, 47, 50
Rotterdam, 35
Rowley, Alec, 43, 64n
Rudland, Malcolm, 80
Ruddles Brewery, 33n
Russell, Ken
  film, 'A Song of Summer', 70

St David's (Dyfed), 79
Savoy Hotel, London, 10
Scholes, Percy, 35
Schönberg, Arnold, 13
Schubert, Franz, 24, 37
  Doppelgänger, Der, 37
  Erlkönig, 37
Schumann, Robert, 12
Scott, Cyril, 44, 52n
  Cuckoo-call, 45
  Danse Nègre, 44
  Lotus Land, 44
  Prelude, 45
Scott, Peter, 75ill
'Seagull of the Land-under-Waves, The', 99
Self, Geoffrey, 42n
Severn, river, 63
Seymour, Miranda, 33n, 64n
Shaw, George Bernard, 90, 91
Shead, Richard, 42n
Shelley, P. B., 73
Shrewsbury School, 63
Skryabin (Scriabin), A., 52n
Skye, 99
Smith, Barry, 14n, 36, 42n
Smith, Olivia ('Viva'), 33n
Sorabji, Kaikhosru, 14, 39, 58
  'Mi Contra Fa', 39
  Piano Concerto, Op 3, 14, 39
South Africa, 19, 89
Southey, Robert, 68

Spencer, Charles, 42n
Spencer, G. T. Leigh, 86
Spicer, Paul
  record, 'Sweet Echo', 80
Stanford, Sir Charles, 93, 95
Stephenson, P. R., 96
  'The Legend of Aleister Crowley', 96
Stevenage, 79
Stevens, Ernest ('Boss-eye'), 31
Stevenson, Ronald, 39
Steyning, 49, 51
Stone, Alby, 64n
Stone House School, 11, 20, 68
Stravinsky, Igor
  Rite of Spring, The, 14
Strong, Rt Rev Thomas B., 57
Stuart-Wortley, Alice (Lady), 12
Suddaby, Elsie, 55
Sudeley, Baron, 18
'Sunday Referee', 51
Swansea, 87
Symonds, John, 53n, 77n, 97ill, 105n
Szigeti, József, 33n

Tanat Valley Light Railway, 68
Taylor, Colin, 29, 64n
Tegid, Llew, 84
Tenby, 90
Terry, Sir Richard, 40, 58
Thatcher, Lady, 42n
Thomas, Dylan, 51, 52, 90
Thornber, Robin, 42n
Tomlinson, Fred, 14n, 51, 59, 76, 98
  'Folk-Song Preludes', introduction, 105n
  'Peter Warlock Handbook, A', 14n, 59, 64n, 105n
  record, 'A Peter Warlock Merry-Go-Down', 98
  'Warlock & Blunt', 64n
  'Warlock & van Dieren', 33n, 42n
'Tôn-y-Botel' (Ebenezer), 20, 78
'Tros y Garreg', 78
Troyes, Chrétien de, 64n

Van Railway, 68
Vaughan-Thomas, Wynford, 68
Vaughan Williams, Ralph, 54, 55, 55ill, 78, 80

115

Wagner, Richard
  Parsifal, 57
Warlock, Peter *see* Heseltine, Philip
Weaver, Helen, 26
Webster, John, 102
Welshpool, 68
West, Ruth, 64n
Whitney-on-Wye, 70, 85
Wilde, Oscar, 44
Williames, Rice Pryce Buckley, 20, 61
Williams, Arthur, 29, 55
Williams, Herbert, 77n
Williams, Ivor, 84

Williams, Mrs J. D. K., 61
Williams, Prof J. E. Caerwyn, 59
Williams, Thomas Jones, 78
Williamson, Malcolm, 80
'Wit & Drollery', 83, 84
Wye, river, 85

Yeats, W. B., 9, 28, 50, 70, 100
  'Grania & Diarmid', 50
Young, Dr Percy M., 12, 14n
  'Elgar, O. M.', 14n, 92n
  'History of British Music, A', 24
  'Letters of Edward Elgar', 77n